Patent Trial Advocacy Casebook

Second Edition

■ ■ ■

Joseph M. Potenza

Christopher J. Renk

Thomas K. Pratt

Erik S. Maurer

Cover design by ABA Publishing.

Printed in the United States of America

14 6 5 4 3 2

Cataloging-in-Publication Data is on file with the Library of Congress.

Patent Trial Advocacy Casebook, Second Edition
Joseph M. Potenza
ISBN: 978-1-60442-753-0

Foreword

As trials become less common today, the need for teaching and enhancing trial skills increases. These course materials are the result of the authors' fifteen years of teaching an advanced course in trial practice geared specifically to a patent infringement trial. They had their genesis in a project for the American Bar Association and National Institute for Trial Advocacy as a program for practicing lawyers; they were refined specifically for undergraduate students at Georgetown University Law Center in Washington, D.C. The authors have now taught the course to more than a hundred law students in small, NITA-style classes. Every aspect of these materials is focused on improving students' proficiency in one event: the trial of a patent case.

The authors are grateful for the contributions made over the years by the students themselves, who have shown remarkable ingenuity and creativity in finding new dimensions to the problems presented here. As patent law has evolved, most particularly through the introduction of the *Markman* practice, so also have the problems, lectures, and course materials.

Each year we experience the joy of watching our students' skills in trial presentation improve, week by week. We now not only see students progress during the course of the semester, but we also see them practice their skills as opposing counsel in real-world litigation. Watching this development is what makes the course fun for the teachers, if not always for the students.

We are grateful for the opportunity to teach this course year after year, to present these revised materials for publication, and most of all to meet and work with the many young professionals who make this labor of love so rewarding.

This edition of *Patent Trial Advocacy Casebook* is dedicated to Mark T. Banner—our deceased partner, friend, and fellow-teacher. Mark was an extraordinary individual: attorney, educator, astute tactician, and patent litigator.

Joseph M. Potenza
Christopher J. Renk
Thomas K. Pratt
Erik S. Maurer

Contents

SECTION

Section A Introduction

The objective of this course is to develop and improve trial skills through "learn-by-doing" techniques. Participants should expect to become more proficient in examining and cross-examining fact and expert witnesses; in handling, authenticating, and introducing documents and other exhibits; and in other trial skills involved in patent litigation. The course is based upon a hypothetical patent infringement controversy that has reached the trial stage. This trial will be a jury trial in Federal Court.

The materials contained in this volume constitute the case file of this patent controversy. All information necessary to prepare for, and participate in, the course is contained in these materials. While the case file is intended to fully portray the patent controversy, the course will not be conducted as a full trial in the traditional sequence. Rather, trial skills will be developed in the context of particular problems that are designed to simulate the courtroom proceedings in various portions of a full trial. Students should consider the issues raised by the facts of the controversy and develop a total trial approach or philosophy.

The course is not designed or intended to be a lecture series on the subject of patent trial advocacy. Each session will consist almost entirely of performances by the participants and critiques by the faculty. This is strictly a "learn-by-doing" approach to instruction. Half of the participants in each group will assume the role of Plaintiff's counsel, and the other half will assume the role of Defendant's counsel. Analysis of the problems from both the plaintiff's and the defendant's points of view is required if offensive and defensive strategies and tactics are to be effective. The setting is intended in all respects to simulate a courtroom atmosphere.

In a typical problem, such as the direct and cross-examination of one of Plaintiff's fact witnesses, a student from Plaintiff's group will be called on to begin direct examination of the witness. During this examination, the other students in the group (including those assigned to represent Plaintiff) may raise appropriate objections to the form or content of the questions asked of the witness. This "all object rule" applies to all trial problems unless otherwise indicated.

After each team has conducted its examinations, the faculty and the other students will critique these individual performances. Students are expected to offer constructive suggestions and discuss the techniques employed.

Except for those problems that specifically deal with the handling and introduction of exhibits, all documents and exhibits are to be treated as already admitted into evidence. Specific instructions are provided for each problem dealing with exhibits.

The necessity for adequate preparation prior to class attendance cannot be overemphasized. There will be little or no time for in-depth preparation during the class; accordingly, all preparations should be completed before arrival. Intimate knowledge of all the facts and familiarity with the supporting documentation is a must. Preparation for conducting the examination of witnesses should involve outlining the areas of their testimony, and preferably, writing out the questions to be asked. Students may refer to their written outlines and questions during examination.

It is essential to devote a substantial portion of the preparation to study of the materials contained in the attached Guide to Trial Advocacy Skills (Exhibit J). This guide includes a discussion of some topics that will be covered at the program, such as opening statements and closing arguments. These topics are included for general information only. The guide is written primarily for jury trials; however, basic considerations are in most instances the same for both bench and jury trials. Faculty members will provide additional insight into considerations unique to patent bench and jury trials, where necessary.

Students should also obtain an up-to-date copy of the Federal Rules of Evidence. Effective participation in the course requires intimate knowledge of the rules relating to the taking of testimony and the offering of exhibits into evidence.

Rules of the United States District Court District of Washington, Western District

Operation of the Court

SECTION B

RULE

1.01 Meetings of the Court; Nature of the Courtroom Experience

The Court is generally in session while Judges of the Court are seated on the bench and Court has been called to order. While the Court is in session, the decorum of the courtroom is to be maintained. Although this is a moot court experience, behavior is expected as though all participants are in a federal courtroom with court called into session.

2.01 Qualifications for Admission to Practice

An applicant for admission to practice before the Court shall have completed all the necessary prerequisites, as may be required by the Court. Only members of the bar of the Court shall be recognized for practice. Attorneys recognized at the podium of the Court shall state their name and the name of the party they represent for the record, unless otherwise directed by Judges of the Court.

3.01 Objections—The "All Object" Rule

The Court utilizes the "All Object" rule. While Court is in session and witnesses are being questioned, all members of the bar of the Court may object to questions.

4.01 Procedure for Objections

Objections under the "All Object" rule are to be made as follows: Any member of the bar of the Court in the role of counsel adverse to the witness examination may orally object at any time, as in federal court. Counsel must object by standing and stating the objection and the rationale for the objection. All other members of the bar of the Court are limited to signifying objection by standing. No one, except the member of the bar in the role of adverse counsel, may be heard on objections, unless called upon by the Court. Except for adverse counsel, the Court will recognize the audience participant objecting at an appropriate time. Once recognized by the Court, the audience participant can state his or her objection and rationale. Until recognized by the Court, the audience participant must remain quiet. The Court retains discretion to bypass objections in the interest of expediting proceedings.

5.01 Procedure on Motions

Specific amounts of time are given to arguments on motions. Counsel is responsible for observing all time limits. All motion hearings shall include oral argument by the movant, opponent, and reply by the movant unless otherwise directed. Counsel is asked to maintain close focus on the issues being considered. Familiarity with the facts of the case is assumed.

6.01 Juries; Juror Qualification Forms

Juror qualification forms shall be confidential. Such forms shall not be made available for inspection by any party and his or her counsel, except upon order of the Chief Judge.

7.01 Exhibits

Exhibits shall be retained by the attorney producing them unless the Court orders them deposited with the Clerk.

8.01 Trial Readiness

Counsel shall be ready for trial when the pertinent case is called to trial. No extensions of time shall be granted.

9.01 Rules of Professional Conduct

The Court hereby adopts as rules of the Court, the Rules of Professional Conduct of the American Bar Association in effect at the time of any subject occurrences.

More specifically, in appearing in a professional capacity before the Court, a lawyer shall not:

(1) make a statement of material fact or law, which the lawyer knows, or reasonably should know, is false;
(2) fail to disclose to the Court a material fact known to the lawyer when disclosure is necessary to avoid assisting in a criminal or fraudulent act by the client;
(3) fail to disclose to the Court legal authority in a controlling jurisdiction known to the lawyer to be directly adverse to the position of the client and not disclosed by opposing counsel;

(4) offer evidence that the lawyer knows to be false, or if the lawyer has offered material evidence and comes to know of its falsity, the lawyer shall take reasonable remedial measures;
(5) participate in the creation or preservation of evidence when the lawyer knows, or reasonably knows, the evidence is false;
(6) intentionally degrade a witness or other person by stating or alluding to personal facts concerning that person, which are not relevant to the case;
(7) in trial,
  (a) allude to any matter that the lawyer does not reasonably believe is relevant, or that will not be supported by admissible evidence,
  (b) assert personal knowledge of facts in issue, except when testifying as a witness, or
  (c) state a personal opinion as to the justness of a cause, the credibility of a witness, or the culpability of a civil litigant;

  however, a lawyer may argue, on analysis of evidence, for any position or conclusion with respect to the matter stated therein; or
(8) refuse to accede to reasonable requests of opposing counsel that do not prejudice the rights of the client.

10.01 Soliciting, Loitering, and Picketing

Soliciting and loitering in the courtroom environs is prohibited. Picketing or parading outside the courtroom is prohibited only when such picketing or parading obstructs or impedes the orderly administration of justice.

Section C Summary of Facts

In the summer of 1995, George L. Parrish and Charley A. Cooley designed and constructed several leveling instruments of the type used in the construction trade by carpenters, bricklayers, cabinetmakers, and the like. One portion of the level was extensible with respect to another portion to permit a length adjustment of the level. The level included a locking feature which immobilized the two portions of the level with respect to each other, when desired.

The original general concept was probably that of George Parrish. The details of the design were worked out by Charley Cooley, although some modification was subsequently necessary when George Parrish actually attempted to construct the first working model. After the first model was constructed, several additional identical levels were constructed and given to the crew chiefs of Parish Construction Company. A few of these levels were also used by marketing people to obtain feedback on the new design from stores in several cities in the United States. At the time these levels were constructed, George Parrish was president of Parrish Construction, while Charley Cooley was vice-president of planning and design.

After several months, the crew chiefs expressed their satisfaction with the new adjustable level, so on March 20, 1996 a patent application was filed by George Parrish and Charley Cooley (Serial Number 452,879). Realizing that they, themselves, would probably not be able to commercially exploit this invention to its fullest, George Parish contacted Bullivant Tool, Inc. of Chicago, a small, but respected, quality tool maker, for possible license or sale of the idea, including the patent rights. Bullivant was then marketing an extensible level, model B-100, under U.S. Patent No. 5,351,524. After some negotiation, an agreement was reached, and the application, which was about to issue, and all the patent rights were assigned to Bullivant Tool. Under the Agreement, George and Charley would each receive a quarterly payment of 5 percent of the wholesale price of each level.

A summary of the prosecution of the application in the Patent Office is located in DX-2. The first office action rejected the patent application as anticipated under 35 U.S.C. § 102(b) in view of the Bullivant U.S. Patent No. 5,351,524. The claims were amended to overcome the rejection. This application issued on April 22, 1997 as U.S. Patent No. 5,624,056.

George L. Parrish was born on April 26, 1957. After graduating from high school on May 22, 1975, George served four years in the United States Army as enlisted personnel in the Corps of Engineers stationed in Germany. He was discharged from the Army on September 3, 1979. He then joined the family business, Parrish Construction Company, as a construction crew chief and worked in various positions in the company. In 1991, George became president of the company upon the retirement of his father, Lamar Parrish.

On February 18, 1999, George L. Parrish died of injuries suffered in an accident at a construction site. His co-inventor and lifelong friend, Charley A. Cooley, succeeded him as president of Parrish Construction Company. The name of the company was subsequently changed to Cooley-Parrish Construction, Inc., of Columbus, Ohio. George's wife, Sue Parrish, was named as executrix of George's Estate.

While on vacation in Jellystone National Park in August 1999 Glen Eakin, vice-president of Bullivant Tool, discovered an adjustable-length level in a local hardware store. The level was designated model PMC-20 and indicated that the manufacturer was the Pacific Machine Corporation of Renton, Washington. This level was similar to the commercial model B-150A produced by Bullivant Tool, incorporating the features of the Parrish-Cooley design. Mr. Eakin purchased the PMC-20 level and brought it to the attention of David W. Horton, president of Bullivant Tool. Mr. Horton discussed the matter with Glen Eakin and decided that a letter should be written to Pacific Machine concerning its model PMC-20. Mr. Horton wrote this letter on September 27, 1999 and enclosed a copy of the Parrish-Cooley patent. A copy of the letter was forwarded to Bullivant's attorney.

The letter was received by Mr. Pringle, president of Pacific Machine Corporation, who in turn distributed copies of the letter to Stu Nellis, director of sales, Alan C. (Ace) Edgar, chief engineer, and Pete Lamp, production manager, who, incidentally, was a registered patent agent. At a subsequent meeting of these four, it was established that the PMC-20 level was designed by Ace Edgar and that first sales of the PMC-20 had occurred in June 1996. It was unanimously agreed by all at the meeting that none of them had previously known of the Parrish-Cooley patent. It was noted that several structural differences existed between the Pacific Machine PMC-20 and the level illustrated in the patent. Pete Lamp suggested that, in view of these differences, Pacific Machine should do nothing and, hopefully, the problem would go away. This course of action was followed, not so much because of Pete Lamp's suggestion, but rather, in the interest of expediency amid other pressing business matters.

Bullivant Tool did not file suit for patent infringement against Pacific Machine until April 20, 2004. During discovery, Bullivant Tool produced an e-mail from Sue Parrish to Charlie Cooley dated December 10, 2004 to which was attached a letter dated October 7, 1979. The 1979 letter was written to George Parrish by his Grandfather, and it included a discussion about an adjustable-length level. Grandpa Parrish, whose first name also was "George," is deceased.

Except as otherwise noted in the Problems, the only witnesses available for trial are those listed on the attached witness list.

Section D

List of Witnesses to Be Called at Trial

Plaintiff Bullivant Tool, Inc. will call the following witnesses:

1. Charley A. Cooley
2. Glen E. Eakin
3. Stuart N. Nellis
4. George W. Marshal (Expert)

Defendant Pacific Machine Corporation will call the following witnesses:

1. Alan C. Edgar
2. Susan S. Parrish
3. Robert M. Johnson (Expert)

Section E Problems

Problem 1 (Basic Direct and Cross-Examination)

Plaintiff has called Charley A. Cooley as its first witness.

(a) For the plaintiff, conduct a direct examination of Mr. Cooley.
(b) For the defendant, conduct a cross-examination of Mr. Cooley.

Problem 2 (Basic Direct and Cross-Examination)

Defendant has called Alan C. Edgar as its first witness.

(a) For the defendant, conduct a direct examination of Mr. Edgar.
(b) For the plaintiff, conduct a cross-examination of Mr. Edgar.

Problem 3 (Basic Direct and Cross-Examination)

Plaintiff has called Glen E. Eakin as its second witness.

(a) For the plaintiff, conduct a direct examination of Mr. Eakin.
(b) For the defendant, conduct a cross-examination of Mr. Eakin.

Problem 4 (Basic Direct and Cross-Examination)

For purposes of this problem only, assume that PMC has obtained a patent on their PMC-20 level. The patent names Alan C. Edgar as the sole inventor, states that PMC is the assignee, and lists both the '524 and '056 Bullivant patents as prior art.

(a) For the defendant, continue direct examination of Mr. Edgar based upon these facts.
(b) For the plaintiff, continue cross-examination of Mr. Edgar based upon these facts.

Problem 5 (Exhibits)

Plaintiff wants to establish the structural details of the allegedly infringing level made and sold by Pacific Machine Corporation.

(a) For the plaintiff, offer the blueprint depicting Defendant's PMC-20 level (PX-7) into evidence and prove that the blueprint accurately portrays the allegedly infringing level. You may use any witnesses you desire to lay a foundation and authenticate the exhibit.
(b) For the defendant, oppose the offer.

Problem 6 (Exhibits)

Defendant wants to establish the investments it made in reliance on the inaction of Plaintiff, subsequent to receipt of the notice of infringement dated September 27, 1999.

(a) For the defendant, offer the memo of January 7, 2005 (DX-9), summarizing Defendant's growth and expansion into evidence. You may use any witnesses you desire to lay a foundation and authenticate the exhibit.
(b) For the plaintiff, oppose the offer.

Problem 7 (Advanced Direct and Cross-Examination—Adverse Witness)

Defendant has called Susan S. Parrish as its second witness.

(a) For the defendant, conduct a direct examination of Ms. Parrish.
(b) For the plaintiff, conduct a cross-examination of Ms. Parrish.

Problem 8 (Advanced Direct and Cross-Examination—Exhibits)

Defendant wants to establish as prior art, the level described in the letter dated October 7, 1979 from Grandpa Parrish to George Parrish (DX-4). Defendant has engaged Sue Parrish to lay the foundation and authenticate the exhibit.

(a) For the defendant, offer the letter of October 7, 1979 into evidence.
(b) For the plaintiff, oppose the offer.

Problem 9 (Advanced Direct and Cross-Examination—Adverse Witness)

Plaintiff has called Stuart Nellis as its third witness.

(a) For the plaintiff, conduct a direct examination of Mr. Nellis.
(b) For the defendant, conduct a cross-examination of Mr. Nellis.

Problem 10 (Advanced Direct and Cross-Examination—Impeachment)

Assume that at trial Susan Parrish has testified on direct-examination that Grandpa "always appeared to understand the difference between reality and fantasy."

(a) For the plaintiff, impeach Ms. Parrish.
(b) For the defendant, conduct a redirect examination of Ms. Parrish.

Problem 11 (Experts—Witness Will Be Provided)

Assume that Mr. Marshal has *not* been qualified as an expert by stipulation.

(a) For the plaintiff, qualify Mr. Marshal and conduct his direct examination.
(b) For the defendant, oppose his qualification and cross-examine him.

Problem 12 (Experts—Witness Will Be Provided)

Assume that Dr. Johnson *has* been qualified as an expert.

(a) For the defendant, conduct a direct examination of Dr. Johnson.
(b) For the plaintiff, cross-examine Dr. Johnson.

Section F Selected Pleadings

SECTION F-1

IN THE UNITED STATES DISTRICT COURT
DISTRICT OF WASHINGTON

BULLIVANT TOOL, INC.	)	
	)	
(an Illinois corporation)	)	
	)	
Plaintiff,	)	Case No. 04 9876
	)	
PACIFIC MACHINE CORPORATION	)	Jury Trial Demanded
	)	
(a Delaware corporation)	)	
	)	
Defendant.	)	

COMPLAINT

Plaintiff, Bullivant Tool, Inc. ("BT"), by its attorneys, for its complaint against Defendants, Pacific Machine Corporation, hereby demands a jury trial and alleges as follows:

NATURE OF THE ACTION

1. This is an action for patent infringement arising under 35 U.S.C. § 81 et. seq.

PARTIES INVOLVED

2. Plaintiff, Bullivant Tool, Inc. is a corporation organized and existing under the laws of the State of Illinois, having its principal place of business at 135 LaSalle Street, Chicago, Illinois 60603.

3. Pacific Machine Corporation is a corporation organized and existing under the laws of the State of Delaware, having a regular and established place of business within this District at 230 Airport Way, Renton, Washington 98055.

JURISDICTION AND VENUE

4. This Court has exclusive jurisdiction of this action pursuant to 28 U.S.C. § 1338(a), and venue is properly laid in this District pursuant to 28 U.S.C. §§ 1400(b).

5. This Court has personal jurisdiction over Defendants. Defendants are doing business in this district. Upon information and belief, Defendants have offered for sale products to be used in accordance with the claims of the patent in suit.

COUNT I

6. On April 22, 1997 United States Letters Patent No. 5,624,056 (hereinafter "the `056 patent") was duly and legally issued to George L. Parrish and Charley A. Cooley for an Adjustable Plumb and Level. A copy of the `056 patent is attached hereto as Exhibit A.

7. Plaintiff is the owner of all right, title, and interest in the `056 patent.

8. Upon information and belief, Defendant has been, and is still, infringing the `056 patent by making, using, or selling, within this District and elsewhere, levels which embody the patented invention, namely Defendant's Model PMC-20 and possibly others, and will continue to do so unless enjoined by this Court.

9. Upon information and belief, Defendant's infringement of the `056 patent has been willful and deliberate, notice of Plaintiff's patent number having been duly placed on all of Plaintiff's devices since the issuance of the `056 patent, and the Defendant having been made aware of the `056 patent by a letter sent September 27, 1999 via U.S. Mail.

10. The infringement by Defendant of the `056 patent has deprived Plaintiff of sales of levels which it otherwise would have made, and has in other respects injured Plaintiff and will cause Plaintiff added injury and loss of profits unless enjoined by this Court.

WHEREFORE Plaintiff prays that his Court:

(a) Issue preliminary and permanent injunctions against continued infringement, inducement of infringement, and contributory infringement by Defendant;

(b) Order an accounting for damages caused by Defendant and order that such damages be trebled because of the Defendant's willful and deliberate infringement;

(c) Order an assessment of interest, costs, and reasonable attorney's fees against the Defendant; and

(d) Order such other and further relief as the Court may deem just.

Date: April 20, 2004

Amos A. Adams

Amos A. Adams
ARUNDEL & ADAMS
Attorneys for Plaintiff
1000 Japan Trade Building
Seattle, Washington 98120
Phone: 206-354-2400

SECTION F-2

IN THE UNITED STATES DISTRICT COURT
DISTRICT OF WASHINGTON

BULLIVANT TOOL, INC.	)	
	)	
(an Illinois corporation)	)	
	)	
Plaintiff,	)	Case No. 04 9876
	)	
PACIFIC MACHINE CORPORATION	)	Jury Trial Demanded
	)	
(a Delaware corporation)	)	
	)	
Defendant.	)	

ANSWER

Defendant, Pacific Machine Corporation, by its undersigned attorneys, answers the Complaint herein as follows:

1. Defendant admits to the allegations of ¶ 2 of the Complaint.

2. Defendant has insufficient knowledge or information to form a belief as to the allegations of ¶ 1 of the Complaint, and therefore denies the same.

3. Defendant admits to the allegations of ¶ 3 of the Complaint.

4. Defendant admits to the allegations of ¶ 4 of the Complaint.

5. Defendant admits to the allegations of ¶ 5 of the Complaint.

6. Defendant admits that Unites States Letters Patent No. 5,624,056 (hereinafter "the `056 patent") was issued on April 22, 1997. Defendant specifically denies that the `056 patent was duly and legally issued.

7. Defendant is without sufficient knowledge or information to form a belief as to Plaintiff's ownership of the `056 patent and therefore denies the allegation of ¶ 7 of the Complaint.

8. As to ¶ 8 of the Complaint, Defendant admits that it has manufactured and sold levels identified as model PMC-20, but specifically denies that these, or any other levels manufactured or sold by Defendant, infringe the `056 patent.

9. As to ¶ 9 of the Complaint, Defendant admits having received a letter from Plaintiff in the Fall of 1999, which brought the `056 patent to Defendant's attention. Defendant specifically denies that it had infringed the `056 patent in any manner. Defendant is without sufficient knowledge or information to form a belief as to the remaining allegations of this paragraph, and therefore denies the same.

10. Defendant denies the allegations of ¶ 10 of the Complaint.

11. Defendant denies each and every allegation of the Complaint not hereinabove admitted, controverted, or denied.

AFFIRMATIVE DEFENSES

To further answer the Complaint, and as affirmative defenses to the matters set forth therein, Defendant alleges on information and belief that:

I.

(Invalidity)

United States Letters Patent No. 5,624,056 is invalid, unenforceable, and void for one or more of the following reasons:

(a) The alleged invention of the `056 patent was known or used by others in this country before the invention thereof by the applicants for the `056 patent [35 U.S.C. § 102(a)];

(b) The alleged invention of the `056 patent was patented, or in public use, or on sale in this country, more than one-year prior to the date of the application for patent in the United States [35 U.S.C. § 102(b)];

(c) The applicants for the `056 patent did not themselves invent the subject matter patented [35 U.S.C. § 102(f)];

(d) Before the applicants' alleged invention thereof, the invention was made in this country by another who had not abandoned, suppressed, or concealed it [35 U.S.C. § 102(g)];

(e) The differences between the subject matter patented and the prior art are such that the subject matter as a whole would have been obvious at the time the alleged invention was made to a person having ordinary skill in the art to which said subject matter pertains [35 U.S.C. § 103];

(f) the applicants failed to disclose the best mode of the invention as required by 35 U.S.C. § 112.

II.

(Laches and Estoppel)

Plaintiff unreasonably and inexcusably delayed instituting this action, which delay resulted in prejudice to Defendant. Defendant received the letter from Plaintiff referred to in paragraph 9 of this Answer, but Plaintiff engaged in conduct during said period of delay, which misled Defendant into believing that Plaintiff had abandoned the patent in suit or acquiesced in the alleged infringement. Defendant relied to its detriment on such conduct of Plaintiff by increased investment in the expansion of its business during said period of delay. The patent is, therefore, unenforceable against Defendant.

III.

(Non-Infringement)

Defendant does not infringe any claim of the `056 patent either directly, indirectly, contributorily, through the doctrine of equivalents, or otherwise.

WHEREFORE, Defendant requests:

(a) That Plaintiff's Complaint be dismissed;

(b) That judgment be entered declaring United States Letters Patent No. 5,624,056 invalid, void, and unenforceable, and that Defendant has not infringed said patent;

(c) That Plaintiff be enjoined from instituting, prosecuting, or threatening to bring any civil action or proceeding of any nature whatsoever based upon said patent against anyone, including this Defendant;

(d) That costs and reasonable attorneys' fees be assessed against Plaintiff; and

(e) That this Defendant be awarded such other and further relief as may be just and equitable under the circumstances.

Date: ______________________

Charles F. Jetsam
FLOTSAM & JETSAM
Attorneys for Defendant
98765 Ocean Avenue
Seattle, Washington 98120
(206) 354-2800

SECTION F-3

IN THE UNITED STATES DISTRICT COURT
DISTRICT OF WASHINGTON

BULLIVANT TOOL, INC.	)	
	)	
(an Illinois corporation)	)	
	)	
Plaintiff,	)	Case No. 04 9876
	)	
PACIFIC MACHINE CORPORATION	)	Jury Trial Demanded
	)	
(a Delaware corporation)	)	
	)	
Defendant.	)	

Written Report of Plaintiff's Expert,
George W. Marshal, Pursuant to Rule 26(a)(2)

I, George W. Marshal as an expert witness for the plaintiff, BULLIVANT TOOL, INC., and pursuant to the Federal Rules of Civil Procedure, Rule 26(a)(2), state as follows:

1. I received a Bachelor of Science Degree in Mechanical Engineering from Purdue University in 1975.

2. From approximately July 1, 1975 until June 30, 1995 I was employed as a Patent Examiner in the United States Patent and Trademark Office. For a period commencing in 1975 and ending approximately January 1992 I was assigned to Group Art Unit 323 or its predecessor, and had responsibility for the examination of patent applications throughout Class 81, which includes hand tools.

3. From approximately February 1992 through June 1995 I was assigned to Group Art Unit 243 where my responsibilities included examination of patent applications in Class 33, Geometrical Instruments, and more specifically to Subclasses 365 et. seq., which include adjustable level devices. I retired from the Patent Office on or about July 4, 1995. I am presently self-employed as a patent searcher.

4. Within the past ten years, I have authored "The Preamble as a Claim Limitation," THE PATENT SOCIETY JOURNAL, Vol. 15, No. II (1993); 'The Thorough Examination—Searching The Interference Files," THE PATENT SOCIETY JOURNAL, Vol. 14, No.4 (1992); and "How to Succeed in Today's United States Patent and Trademark Office," GOVERNMENT TODAY AND TOMORROW, Vol. 12, Issue 5 (1989).

5. I have received to date $40,834.27 in compensation for my opinion study and testimony in this litigation.

6. Within the preceding four years, I have testified as an expert by deposition in *Marberg, Inc. v. Neiltor Co.* I have not testified as an expert at trial within the past four years.

7. I have been retained by Bullivant Tool Inc. as an expert witness in this action. I expect to offer testimony concerning my knowledge and expert opinions regarding the technology at issue in this case.

8. I have been informed that determining infringement is a two-step process. First, the words in the asserted claims are construed to determine what they mean to one of ordinary skill. In construing claims, the terms in the claims are normally given their plain and ordinary meaning, unless the patentee offers a clear disavowal, in the

specification or during prosecution, indicating that a different definition is to be used. In the second step, the properly construed claim is compared to the accused product.

9. I have been informed that there are several ways that an accused product can infringe a patent claim. The first, known as "literal" infringement, occurs when the accused product or method has each and every element (or performs each and every step) specified in the properly construed claim. That is, if all of the elements of the claim are present, literal infringement is present.

10. I have further been informed that a determination that there is no literal infringement does not end an infringement inquiry. If an accused device or method lacks a claim limitation, it may still infringe under the doctrine of equivalents. I understand that the application of the doctrine of equivalents rests on the substantiality of the differences between the claimed device and the accused product. If the accused product is insubstantially different from the claimed device, then the product may be considered an equivalent, and may infringe under the doctrine of equivalents.

11. I have also been informed that in applying the doctrine of equivalents, it is important to assess whether the accused product or process (1) performs substantially the same function, (2) in substantially the same way, to (3) achieve substantially the same result as the claimed product or process.

12. I will testify as to the infringing character of Defendant's extensible level. In my opinion, the Defendant's level model PMC-20 infringes the claims of the patent in suit literally and under the Doctrine of Equivalents. My opinion that Defendant's level model PMC-20 infringes the claims of the patent in suit is based on the claim comparison contained in Exhibit A attached hereto.

13. In arriving at my conclusions, I have reviewed the `056 patent (PX-l), its prosecution history, including the art cited therein (Bullivant, U.S. Patent No. 5,351,524 (DX-l)). Further, I have examined a Pacific Machine Corporation extensible level, PMC-20 (PX-8), and a blueprint of the PMC-20 extensible level, Drawing No. 20-01-1C (PX-7).

I declare the foregoing is true and correct.

Date: October 21, 2004

George W. Marshal
George W. Marshal

EXHIBIT A

Claim Comparison, U.S. Patent No. 5,624,056

The single patent claim is reproduced below. The numerals in brackets designate the recited elements. These have counterparts in defendant's level, as indicated on the attached drawing. Explanatory notes follow the claim.

> An extensible, non-overlapping plumb and level comprising a body member [I] having channels [II] in the side faces [IIIa, IIIb]* thereof, an extension [IV] disposed for sliding movement on the body member [I], said extension [IV] having arms [V] slidable in the channels [II]** of the body member [I], and locking means [VI] carried by the body member [I] for frictional engagement with the arms [V]*** to selectively prevent movement of the extension [IV].

Notes:

* The side-opening grooves along the top and bottom of the body member of defendant's level are in the "side faces" of the body member I because the side faces include offset surfaces IIIa and IIIb. In any event, the body member I having side-opening grooves between offset surfaces IIIa and IIIb of defendant's level performs substantially the same function in substantially the same way to achieve substantially the same result as that of a body having channels in the side faces thereof, as recited in the claim.

** This recitation is broad enough to encompass the structure of defendant's level, wherein flanges Va of the arms V (rather than the arms in their entirety) are slidable in the channels II. In any event, the flange and arm are equivalent to those recited (*i.e.* "an extension

[IV] disposed for sliding movement on the body member [I], said extension [IV] having arms [VI] slidable in the channels [II]") as recited in the claim.

*** The arrangement in defendant's level of a spring-loaded pin cooperating with spaced holes performs the same function of preventing movement of the extension as recited in the claim. The structure performing that function in the defendant's level (spring-loaded pin cooperating with spaced holes) is the same or an equivalent to the nut, shaft and locking plate arrangement disclosed in the '056 patent.

In any event, the action of the spring-loaded pin (its outer surface) against the walls of the detent creates a frictional engagement which is equivalent to the locking means recited in the claim and the mechanism described in the specification in that in both cases there is resistance to the movement between the two bodies. Here, the defendant's level having the spring-loaded pin (its outer surface) against the walls of the detent performs the same function of selectively preventing movement of the extension, in substantially the same way by using a locking mechanism, to achieve the same result -- prevention of movement of the extension relative to the body member.

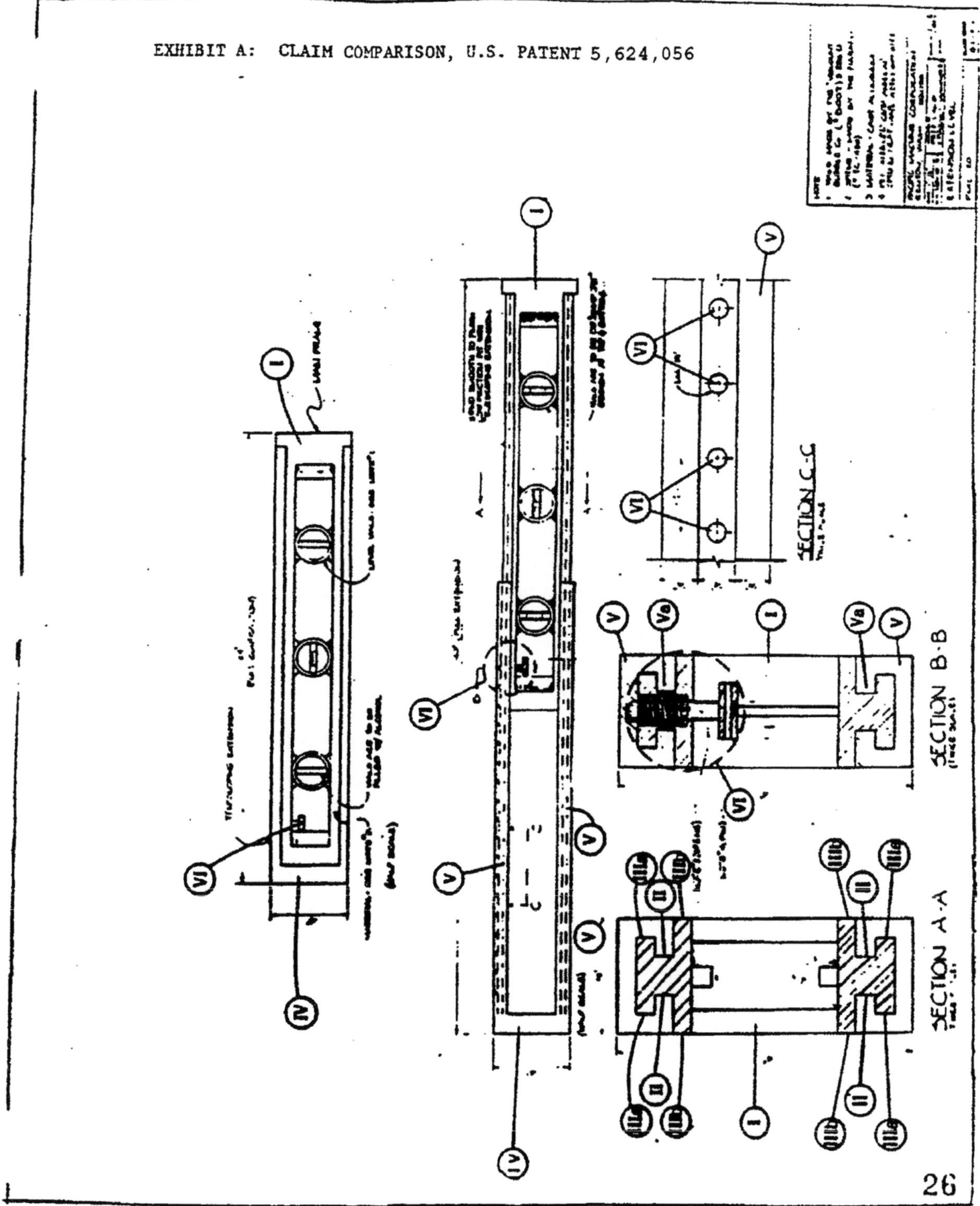
EXHIBIT A: CLAIM COMPARISON, U.S. PATENT 5,624,056
SECTION A-A
SECTION B-B
SECTION C-C
26

SECTION F-4

IN THE UNITED STATES DISTRICT COURT
DISTRICT OF WASHINGTON

BULLIVANT TOOL, INC.	)	
	)	
(an Illinois corporation)	)	
	)	
Plaintiff,	)	Case No. 04 9876
	)	
PACIFIC MACHINE CORPORATION	)	Jury Trial Demanded
	)	
(a Delaware corporation)	)	
	)	
Defendant.	)	

Written Report of Defendant's Expert,
Dr. Robert M. Johnson, Pursuant to Rule 26(a)(2)

I, Dr. Robert M. Johnson, pursuant to Rule 26(a)(2) of the Federal Rules of Civil Procedure, and on behalf of Defendant, Pacific Machine Corporation, will testify that:

Background

1. I received a Ph.D. in Civil Engineering from the Massachusetts Institute of Technology in 1954.

2. I, from 1959 to approximately 1964, served in the United States Army Corps of Engineers. During this service, I was involved in designing and supervising the construction of tactical support structures. In the fall of 1964, I took a position on the faculty of the Civil Engineering Department of Boston University. I remain to this date as a member of the Civil Engineering Department faculty. As a member of the faculty at

Boston University, I have taught numerous engineering courses, primarily in the area of strengths of materials.

3. Over the past approximately fifteen years, I have served as a consultant to a number of tool fabrication companies through the United States Hand Tool Manufacturers Association ("ASTM").

4. I am currently the chairman of the ASTM Committee on Tool Materials.

5. As to this matter, I have received a total of $15,004.00.

6. I have written extensively in the area of materials, and within the last ten years I have written the following articles: (I) "Tempering Steel for Hammer," TOOLS, TOOLS, TOOLS, Vol. 5, Issue 2 (1990); (2) "Elasticity of No. 2 Grade Steel," ELASTICITY OF TODAY'S PRODUCTS, Vol. 50 (1992); (3) "Elasticity of No. 3 Grade Steel," ELASTICITY OF TODAY'S PRODUCTS, Vol. 51 (1992); (4) "Tooling-Up for the Future," TOOLS AND THINGS, Vol. 15, Issue 22 (1998); "Hardening the Hand Tool," *Popular Tooling* (1998).

7. Within the past four years, I have testified in the following suits:

(1) *In re Zelleeni Tool Co., Inc.*;

(2) *Zelleeni Tool Co., Inc. v. Hand Tools of America. Inc.*;

(3) *KruptTool Gesellschaft M.b.H. v. Zelleeni Tool Co., Inc.*;

(4) *Tool-O-Matic Co. of America v. Fujiyama Tool Works*.

8. I have been retained by Pacific Machine Corporation ("PMC") as an expert witness in this action. I expect to offer testimony concerning my knowledge and expert opinions regarding the technology at issue in this case, including the structure and operation of the accused PMC product. I have been asked by PMC to review, among

other documents and testimonial evidence, the `056 patent (PX-I), and its prosecution history.

Patent Validity

9. I am informed that in order for a prior art reference, device, or system to anticipate a claim of a patent, the prior art reference, device, or system must contain or disclose to one of ordinary skill each and every element of the claim. A claim feature can be expressly contained or disclosed. If an express teaching of a claim feature is missing from a reference, it can still be considered inherently disclosed by the reference if the missing feature would necessarily be present in the system/process described in the reference.

10. I am informed that if a prior art reference or device fails to teach, expressly or by inherency, every feature in a claim, then that reference does not anticipate the claim. Such a claim, however, may be invalid for obviousness if the differences between the claim and the prior art are such that the claimed subject matter, as a whole, would have been obvious to one of ordinary skill in the art at the time the claimed invention was made. I am informed that combinations of prior art references may invalidate a patent so long as one of ordinary skill in the art would be motivated to combine such references, and that they would have a reasonable expectation of success in making such a combination. I am informed that these motivations might be based on a suggestion in the references themselves, or what was generally known by those skilled in the art at the time. I understand that before an obviousness determination is made, the level of ordinary skill in the art must be considered, the scope and content of the prior art

must be considered, and the differences between the claimed invention and the prior art must be evaluated. I also understand that secondary considerations of non-obviousness, if present, should be considered in the obviousness determination.

11. I will testify as an expert witness as to the invalidity of the patent in suit. In this regard, I will testify as to: (1) the level of ordinary skill in the art to which the invention of the patent in suit pertains, and (2) the question of obviousness of the alleged invention. The level of ordinary skill in the art is a Bachelor of Science in either Mechanical or Civil Engineering having about three years of experience in designing hand tools. I base my opinion as to the level of ordinary skill in the art on my numerous contacts with design engineers working in the field of the invention, and with senior engineering students at Boston University.

12. I will testify that the alleged invention of the patent in suit would have been obvious to one of ordinary skill in the art from a reading of Bullivant, U.S. Patent No. 5,351,524 (DX-l), either alone or in combination with the public use of an extensible level by George M. Parrish, grandfather of the deceased co-inventor George L. Parrish (DX-4). Bullivant teaches and discloses all of the limitations of the claim of the `056 patent except for the locking means. Implementing a locking means in the extensible level disclosed by Bullivant would have been obvious to one skilled in the art at the time of the invention. Moreover, the claimed invention would have been obvious to one of ordinary skill in the art, based on the extensible level taught by Bullivant in combination with George M. Parrish's extensible level having locking means (DX-4). This opinion is based on my personal knowledge of extensible levels and other adjustable tools containing stop or lock mechanisms.

13. I understand that certain objective factors may bear on the determination of whether the subject matter of the claimed invention was obvious to one of ordinary skill in the art at the time the claimed invention was made. I understand that such factors include: (I) whether there was a long-felt, but unsolved, need for the claimed invention; (II) whether others attempted, but failed, to invent the claimed invention; (III) whether there was copying by others; (IV) whether the claimed invention achieved any unexpected results; and (V) the commercial success, if any, of the claimed invention. I have considered whether any of these factors would contradict my opinion that the `056 patent would have been obvious to one of ordinary skill in the art, and I am not aware of the existence of any of these factors that would contradict my opinion.

Patent Infringement

14. I am informed that a proper analysis of patent infringement involves a two-step process. First, the claims must be properly construed to determine their scope and meaning. In construing claims in a patent, I understand that one must consider the claim language, the patent specification, and the prosecution history to ascertain the meaning that one of ordinary skill in the art would give to the claims. Second, the claims, as properly construed, must be compared to the accused product(s).

15. I am informed that literal infringement of a claim exists when every limitation recited in the claim is found in the accused device or method. That is, when the properly construed claim describes the accused device or method exactly, there is literal infringement. It is my further understanding that literal infringement of a means-plus-function claim limitation under 35 U.S.C. §112(6) requires that the accused device have

the structure disclosed in the specification (or equivalent structure) for performing the identical function recited in the claim.

16. I am further informed that a device that does not literally infringe a claim may still infringe under the doctrine of equivalents if *every* limitation in the claim is literally or equivalently present in the accused product. I understand that a claim limitation is equivalently present in an accused product if only "insubstantial differences" distinguish the missing claim limitation from the corresponding aspects of the accused product. I further understand that the substantiality of each difference is assessed from the vantage point of one of ordinary skill in the relevant art, and that one way of measuring the substantiality of the differences is to examine whether the element of the accused product performs substantially the same function, in substantially the same way, to achieve substantially the same result, as the limitation at issue in the claim.

17. I am further informed that a doctrine known as "prosecution history estoppel" prevents a patentee from reclaiming, through the doctrine of equivalents, claim scope that was surrendered during prosecution. Under prosecution history estoppel, application of the doctrine of equivalents can be limited whenever there is a claim amendment that narrows the scope of the claim, unless the patentee can show that the amendment was made for reasons unrelated to the statutory requirements for patentability. In those cases where the amendment was made for reasons of patentability, the amendment may be presumed to be a general disclaimer of the territory between the original claim and the amended claim. In some cases, the patentee can overcome the presumption (*e.g.*, the patentee must show that at the time of the amendment one skilled in the art could not reasonably be expected to have drafted a claim that would have

literally encompassed the alleged equivalent). These cases include situations wherein: (1) the equivalent may have been unforeseeable at the time of the application; (2) the rationale underlying the amendment may bear no more than a tangential relation to the equivalent in question; and (3) there may be some other reason suggesting that the patentee could not reasonably be expected to have described the insubstantial substitute in question.

18. I will further testify as an expert witness that the defendant's extensible level does not infringe the patent in suit. In this regard, I will testify that defendant's extensible level does not have channels in the side faces of a body member as required by the claim. Further, the defendant's extensible level does not have an equivalent of the channels in side faces.

19. I will testify that the defendant's extensible level does not have arms entirely within the channel as required by the claim. I will also testify that the defendant's extensible level does not have an equivalent of arms entirely within the channel.

20. Further, I will testify that the defendant's extensible level does not infringe the claim of the patent in suit because it does not include locking means for frictionally engaging the arm. The defendant's level does not infringe because the locking means does not engage a plurality of arms as required by the claim of the patent in suit. Nor does the defendant's level have an equivalent to the locking means as recited in the claim of the patent in suit.

21. Further, I will testify that the defendant's extensible level does not infringe the claim of the patent-in-suit because it is not non-overlapping.

22. In arriving at my conclusions, I have reviewed the `056 patent (PX-1) and its prosecution history, including the art cited therein (Bullivant, U.S. Patent No. 5,351,524 (DX-1). Further, I have examined a Pacific Machine Corporation extensible level, PMC-20 (PX-8), and a blueprint of the PMC-20 extensible level, Drawing No. 20-0 I-I C (PX-7). Moreover, I have reviewed a letter dated October 7, 1979 by George M. Parrish, including the accompanying drawing (DX-4).

23. Finally, I will testify that the PMC-20 employs the features found in the prior art as shown by Bullivant (DX-1).

Respectfully submitted,

Date: October 21, 2004

Dr. Robert M. Johnson

SECTION F

SECTION F-5

IN THE UNITED STATES DISTRICT COURT
DISTRICT OF WASHINGTON

BULLIVANT TOOL, INC.	)	
	)	
(an Illinois corporation)	)	
	)	
Plaintiff,	)	Case No. 04 9876
	)	
PACIFIC MACHINE CORPORATION	)	Jury Trial Demanded
	)	
(a Delaware corporation)	)	
	)	
Defendant.	)	

Supplemental Written Report of Plaintiff's Expert,
George W. Marshal. Pursuant to Rule 26(a)(2)

I, George W. Marshal as an expert witness for the Plaintiff, BULLIVANT TOOL, INC., supplement my Written Opinion pursuant to the Federal Rules of Civil Procedure, Rule 26(a)(2) by stating that:

1. I have been informed that a valid patent must disclose and claim something that is new. If a claim of a patent covers, or reads on, that which was already known in the art, then the claim is too broad and must be found invalid.

2. I have further been informed that where a single prior art reference discloses, either expressly or by inherency, each and every element of a claim, that claim is said to be anticipated by the reference, and the claim is invalid under 35 U.S.C. §102. A missing feature can be considered inherent only if those of ordinary skill would have

understood that the missing feature was necessarily present in the system/process being described.

3. I understand that a patent claim is invalid if the subject matter, considered as a whole, would have been obvious to one of ordinary skill in the relevant art, at the time the invention was made. I further understand that obviousness is a legal conclusion to be reached based on factual inquiries of four general categories, *viz.* the scope and content of the prior art, the differences between the claimed invention and the prior art, the level of ordinary skill in the relevant art at the time the invention was made, and if present, any objective evidence of non-obviousness, such as commercial success, long-felt, but unresolved need, failure of others to solve the problem, unexpected results, acquiescence in the patent by others, and whether the same or similar inventions were made independently by others prior to, or at about the same time, as the invention of the subject claims.

4. I will further testify that the patent in suit is not invalid. In this regard, I will testify as to: (l) the level of ordinary skill in the art to which the invention of the patent in suit pertains, and (2) the question of obviousness of the alleged invention. The level of ordinary skill in the art is a person having about five years' experience in the mechanical trades of building construction, carpentry, and/or masonry. I base my opinion as to the level of ordinary skill in the art on my numerous contacts with inventors in this field through my work at the United States Patent and Trademark Office.

5. I will also testify that the alleged invention of the patent in suit would <u>not</u> have been obvious to one of ordinary skill in the art from a reading of Bullivant U.S. Patent No. 5,351,524, either alone or in combination with the public use of an extensible

level by George M. Parrish, grandfather of the deceased co-inventor George L. Parrish. Neither Bullivant (DX-l) nor George M. Parrish's adjustable level (DX-4) teaches or suggests, alone or in combination, the extensible level described and claimed in the `056 patent. Moreover, there is no motivation, teaching, or suggestion to combine Bullivant (DX-l) and George M. Parrish's adjustable level (DX-4) to produce an extensible level as claimed in the `056 patent. I base my opinion on my personal knowledge of extensible levels and other adjustable tools containing stop or lock mechanisms in light of my twenty years of experience as a Patent Examiner in the Patent and Trademark Office.

6. In arriving at my conclusions, I have reviewed the `056 patent (PX-l), Bullivant, U.S. Patent No. 5,351,524 (DX-1), and a letter dated October 7, 1979 by George M. Parrish, including the accompanying drawing (DX-4).

I declare the foregoing is true and correct.

Date: November 22, 2004

George W. Marshal
George W. Marshal

Section G Depositions

SECTION NO. **Page**

SECTION G-1

IN THE UNITED STATES DISTRICT COURT OF WASHINGTON

WESTERN DISTRICT

Bullivant Tool, Inc.,)

Plaintiff,) Case No. 04 9876

v.)

Pacific Machine Corporation)

Defendant.)

VIDEOTAPED DEPOSITION OF CHARLEY A. COOLEY

Tuesday, August 16, 2005

Reported by: Kathy G. Kessling, RPR

The videotaped deposition of Charley A. Cooley, a witness herein, was convened on Monday, August 16, 2004, commencing at 9:08 a.m., at the offices of Flotsam & Jetsam, 98765 Ocean Avenue, Seattle, Washington, 98120, before Kathy Geyne Kessling, Registered Professional Reporter.

SECTION G

APPEARANCES

For Plaintiff:
MR. AMOS A. ADAMS, Esquire
1000 Japan Trade Building
Seattle, Washington 98120
Telephone: 206-354-2400

For Defendant:
CHARLES F. JETSAM, Esquire
Flotsam & Jetsam
98765 Ocean Avenue
Seattle, Washington 98120
Telephone: 206-354-2800

Also present: T.J. Sullivan, Videographer

CONTENTS

EXAMINATION BY	PAGE
Mr. Jetsam	6, 16
Mr. Adams	16, 20

EXHIBITS

No.	DESCRIPTION	PAGE
PX-1	U.S. Patent Number 5,624,056	9
PX-2	Letter dated September 2, 1996, from George Parrish to Bullivant Tool Company	13
PX-4	Assignment dated March 20, 1997	14
DX-3	E-mail dated December 10, 2004 from Sue Parrish to Charley Cooley	17
DX-4	Handwritten letter dated October 7, 1979 from Grandpa Parrish to George Parrish (with accompanying drawing)	18

(Exhibits retained by counsel.)

Page 4

Kessling Deposition Services
206-555-1234

PROCEEDINGS

THE VIDEOGRAPHER: On the record with Tape Number 1 of the videotape deposition of Charley A. Cooley, taken by the Defendant in the matter of Bullivant Tool, Inc., versus Pacific Machine Corporation in the United States District Court for Washington, Eastern District, Case Number 04 9876.

This Deposition is being held at the law offices of Flotsam & Jetsam, 98765 Ocean Avenue, Seattle, Washington, 98120, on August 16, 2004, at approximately 9:08 a.m.

My name is T.J. Sullivan, representing Kessling Deposition Services. I'm a certified legal video specialist.

The court reporter is Kathy Geyne Kessling representing Kessling Deposition Services. I'm a certified court reporter.

Will counsel please introduce themselves and indicate which parties they represent.

MR. JETSAM: I am Charles F. Jetsam, counsel for Pacific Machine Corporation.

MR. ADAMS: And I am Mr. Adams, and I represent Bullivant Tool, Inc.

CHARLEY A COOLEY,

called for examination, having been first duly sworn, was examined and testified as follows;

EXAMINATION BY COUNSEL FOR PACIFIC MACHINE CORPORATION BY MR. JETSAM.

Q. Mr. Cooley, you understand you are under oath?

A. Yes.

Q. If I ask any questions today, that you don't understand, please indicate by telling me you don't understand the question. Fair enough?

A. Yes, that's fine.

Q. If you answer a question, I'm going to assume you understood it, okay?

A. Yes.

Q. Have you ever been deposed before?

A. No I haven't.

Q. Okay, if at any time you need to take a break, please let me know, but the only thing I'll ask is that you don't ask for a break before you've given an answer to a pending question.

If your attorney makes an objection please give him an opportunity to speak it because we have a court reporter here and she needs to take down all the questions and answers and it becomes difficult if two people are speaking at once, okay?

A. Sure, that seems reasonable.

Q. Fine. Can you tell me when you were born, sir?

A. I was born March 5, 1957.

Q. Can you tell me a little bit about your education?
A. From when?
Q. From high school.
A. I graduated from high school on May 22, 1975.
Q. What did you do next?
A. I joined the Army and after basic training served four years in the U.S. Army Corps of Engineers. I served two tours of duty in Germany.
Q. Were you honorably discharged?
A. Yes, I was.
Q. When?
A. I was discharged from the Army on July 19, 1979. And yes, it was an honorable discharge.
Q. What did you do next?
A. I went to college.
Q. Where?
A. Ohio State University.
Q. When did you start?
A. Right after I got out of the Army, in the fall of 1979. I had about a month off.
Q. Did you go under the GI Bill?
A. Yes I did. The Army paid for my college education.
Q. What did you study?

A. I studied architectural engineering.
Q. Did you get a degree in architectural engineering?
A. Yes I did.
Q. When?
A. May 29, 1983.
A. What did you do after graduation?
A. I took a job with the Parrish Construction Company.
Q. What was your job?
A. I was a designer.
Q. When did you start at Parrish?
A. Shortly after graduation, I don't remember exactly when, but it was in 1983.
Q. For how long were you a designer?
A. Well, I consider myself a designer to this day because I have those skills. My job changed in title and my duties expanded in 1986 when I became Vice President for Planning and Design.
Q. Do you recall when in 1986?
A. No I really don't.
Q. Is that your title now?
A. No it is not, I'm now President of the company.
Q. When did you become President?
A. In 1999 shortly after George died.

Q. Who is George?

A. George L. Parrish. He was the President of the company.

Q. How well did you know Mr. Parrish?

A. I knew him very well. We had gone to high school together and were on the same football team. Then we joined the Army together and most of the time served in the same unit. He was in the Corps of Engineers as well. He was a good friend and great guy to work for.

Q. Mr. Cooley I'd now like to ask you some questions about a document I'm marking as Plaintiff's Exhibit 1. It is U.S. Patent Number 5,624,056, issued April 22, 1997. Do you recognize Plaintiff's Exhibit 1?

(Plaintiff's Exhibit Number 1 marked for identification.)

A. Yes, of course.

Q. What is it?

A. It's the patent that George and I got.

Q. When you say George?

A. George Parrish. Mr. Parrish and I obtained this patent.

Q. It's the patent in suit that is the subject of this lawsuit, isn't that correct?

A. Yes it is.
Q. Okay. What can you tell me about the idea that led to this patent?
A. Well the original idea concerning the extendable level is George's - Mr. Parrish's. We worked together on perfecting the design for a number of weeks.
Q. What did you do?
A. Well the two of us made three or four replicas of the first working model and we tinkered with the design quite a bit to get it just right.
Q. What did you do with the working models?
A. After we made them we gave them to the crew chiefs of our construction company. We wanted them to use them and see how they worked.
Q. What did you learn?
A. Generally we learned that the crew chiefs liked them a lot. They thought they were very helpful in our kind of work where we frequently are checking the levels of things that run quite an expanse.
Q. How did the patent come about?
A. Well, after the crew chiefs expressed their enthusiasm for our design I thought it would be good idea to see about getting a patent.

SECTION G

Q. What happened next?
A. Well, I talked to George, Mr. Parrish, and he said if it didn't cost too much we should look into it, which is what we did. You know, we went to a patent attorney and he got the patent for us.
Q. What did you show the attorney?
MR.ADAMS. Objection. Privileged.
Mr. Jetsam: Let me rephrase the question. After you first went to the attorney, the patent attorney, what did you do?
A. Well, of course, it took quite a while for us to get the patent. But we gave him some money and in a few months he gave us a patent application, which we signed and, I don't remember the timing or anything, later on we got our patent.
Q. Let me change subjects for a minute. I'd like to get some sense of the time when all of this happened. When did you and Mr. Parrish design the level depicted in your patent?
A. We worked on it in the summer of 1995. I remember it was in early June that we began the design because school was just getting out and we were hiring a bunch of summer kids for the company. We were talking about finding a way to make a level that would be more accurate on these long rungs of wood.
Q. Do you have a sense of how long it took you?

A. Well, it was over the course of the summer that we designed and constructed the prototype of this level. By the time school was back, say in September or October, I know we were done by then. We'd already begun to give at least some of the early prototypes to the crew chiefs to evaluate.

Q. According to the patent you filed the application on March 20, 1996. Is that right?

A. I don't really know, I assume it's right. That's what was all handled by the patent attorney.

Q. When were you talking to the patent attorney?

A. Well it had to be in the fall and winter of 1995, 1996. After we got the design down the way we wanted it, that's when I had the idea we should consider patenting it. It took a little while to find the attorney and do that stuff, but not that much time. But with the holidays and all I can't be sure exactly when.

Q. How long after filing . . .
Strike that.

Q. After filing for the patent, what did you do?

A. Well, after we had the patent on file, George thought it would be a good idea to try to get someone to make the levels for us. We're a construction company not a tool company, so we went to one of the best tool companies in the business. George

SECTION G

went to Bullivant Tool and tried to see if they would be interested in making them for us and paying us some kind of money in return.

Q. Why did you pick Bullivant Tool?

A. Well, it was the Cadillac of the industry. It made an extension level that was one of the best.

Q. How did you know about the Bullivant extension level?

A. We'd been giving them as gifts to our crew chiefs.

Q. On what occasion would you give them as gifts?

A. After they'd completed three years of service. Our design was actually better than the Bullivant model, and we thought they might be interested in making the improved model.

Q. I'd like to show you what's been marked as Plaintiff's Exhibit 2. It is a letter dated September 2, 1996, from George Parrish to Bullivant Tool. Do you recognize that letter?

(Plaintiff's Exhibit Number 2 marked for identification.)

A. Yes I do.

Q. How do you recognize it?

A. Well this was our invention. We talked about approaching Bullivant and George - Mr. Parrish - as President of the company wrote to Bullivant Tool to see if they would be interested in our invention. This is what I was talking about.

Q. Did you see this letter on or about the time it was sent?

A. Yes. I saw it before it was sent and I saw it at the time it was sent. George and I were together, in fact, when he signed it. We didn't want to tell anyone about our improvement until after we'd learned that our patent was going to issue from the Patent Office. I remember we kept it secret until after we had that information.

Q. You say you kept it secret. You did tell your crew chiefs about them, didn't you?

A. Of course, in fact we gave them some. We'd been using them in the business. But by "secret" I meant we didn't try to interest anyone in the patent until after we knew it would be approved.

Q. Was this letter kept by Parrish Construction Company in the ordinary course of business?

A. Yes. We had a file on this invention issue and this was in the file. Of course we kept it.

Q. I'm going to show you a document marked as Plaintiff's Exhibit 4. It is entitled Assignment and is dated March 20, 1997. Do you recognize this document?

(Plaintiff's Exhibit Number 4 marked for identification.)

A. Yes I do.
Q. What is it?
A. This is the document where we gave the patent to Bullivant.
Q. Do you recognize the signatures on the second page?
A. Well, I recognize George Parrish's signature and certainly I recognize my signature. Down on the bottom is the signature of a notary, and I remember her signing it but I don't recognize her signature per se.
Q. So this is the assignment document that you and Mr. Parrish signed?
A. Yes. We signed it together.
Q. I note that the document says that you received a dollar to assign your patent application to Bullivant. Is that correct?
A. Well, yes, but I think the dollar is just some legal thing. We were given a royalty for every one of the patented levels that Bullivant sold. So the dollar was just, you know, for the agreement.
Q. Did this assign the patent that you obtained to Bullivant?
A. Yes. This was just before the patent came out, and after we knew it was going to issue. So we assigned it to

Bullivant and Bullivant was going to make the level and we were going to get a royalty for every one they sold.

Q. And the patent we're referring to is the `056 patent in suit, marked as Plaintiff's Exhibit 1?

A. Yes.

Q. And here you can see it issued on April 22, 1997.

A. It was just about a month after we made this assignment.

Q. Can you tell me how much royalty you receive for each sale of one of your levels.

A. Sure. Our agreement is that each of us receive 5% of the wholesale price when Bullivant sells a level.

Q. When you say each of you what to you mean?

A. Well, George Parrish would get 5% and I would get 5%. Now, of course, it goes to his widow, Sue Parrish.

Q. When did Mr. Parrish die?

A. He had an unfortunate accident in 1999, on February 18. He died of injuries on an accident at one of our construction sites. It was right before I became President. That's when we changed the name of the company from Parrish Construction to Cooley-Parrish Construction.

Q. Have you received royalties under your agreement with Bullivant?

A. Yes. Every quarter we get a report on the number of tools they sold, the dollars they sold them for, and how much we're due. A check comes with the report, just like clockwork.

Q. By "we," who do you mean?

A. Well, me and Sue Parrish. We each got equal amounts. 5% each.

Q. No further questions.

CROSS EXAMINATION BY MR. ADAMS.

Q. Mr. Cooley, I'd like to show you what's been marked as Defendant's Exhibit 3. It is an e-mail dated December 10, 2004. Do you recognize this?

(Defendant's Exhibit Number 3 marked for identification.)

A. Yes.

Q. What is it?

A. It's an e-mail from Sue Parrish to me.

Q. Why did she send that e-mail?

MR. JETSAM: Objection. Calls for speculation.

A. I don't really know, you would have ask her.

Q. Did you receive this e-mail on December 10, 2004.

A. Yes.

Q. Did you talk to Mrs. Parrish about it?

A. No, I don't think so.

Q. Why not?
A. It seemed pretty self-explanatory. I don't know, it just didn't seem that I needed to talk to her about anything.
Q. Defendant's Exhibit 3 refers to a letter that she says she attached and that came from her late husband's grandfather. Is that correct?
A. Yes.
Q. I'm showing you what I've marked as Defendant's Exhibit 4, a handwritten letter dated October 7, 1979. Do you recognize that?
(Plaintiff's Exhibit Number 4 marked for identification.)
A. Yes, it's the letter Sue Parrish sent with the e-mail.
Q. You mean Defendant's Exhibit 3?
A. Yes. She wrote Defendant's Exhibit 3 and sent me this.
Q. Defendant's Exhibit 4.
A. Yes, Defendant's Exhibit 4.
Q. Had you ever seen Defendant's Exhibit 4 before?
A. No.
Q. Do you recognize it as being a letter from Mr. Parrish's grandfather to Mr. Parrish.
A. Not really.

SECTION G

Q. Are you aware of Mr. Parrish's grandfather's handwriting?
A. No, I don't think so.
Q. Have you ever met Mr. Parrish's grandfather?
A. Yes, I met him once or twice.
Q. What do you remember about him?
A. Nothing really. He was a kindly, old, white-haired gentleman, but I don't have a strong recollection other than that.
Q. Would you take a moment to read Defendant's Exhibit 4 please and tell me whether the content of that letter is true?
MR. JETSAM: Lacks foundation.
Q. Tell me whether you have any personal knowledge about the contents of that letter.
A. Not really. I mean I know George Parrish returned from Germany and the Army because he came back around the time I did, but as to the other stuff about the level, I have no knowledge at all.
Q. Part of the letter, the last page, is a drawing. Do you see that?
A. Yes.
Q. Had you ever seen that drawing before?
A. No.

Q. The first time you saw it was when Mrs. Parrish sent it to you?
A. Yes.
Q. Did Mr. Parrish ever mention it to you?
A. No.
Q. Did Mr. Parrish ever mention to you that his grandfather had designed an extensible level?
A. No.
Q. Was Mr. Parrish close to his grandfather?
A. I don't really know. I mean he was a nice guy, as far as I could tell, but he didn't live with them or anything like that.
Q. I'd like to change topics to the four levels that you made as prototypes. You said they were given to crew chiefs, right?
A. Yes.
Q. Can you tell me who they are?
A. Well, it's been a while. One was Carl Behrens, another was Larry DeFazio, the third was Ramon Garcia, and I think the fourth was Jim Hadley. I think Jim was a crew chief back then.
Q. Are these people still employed by your company?
A. Two of them are. Carl and Jim.

Q. Mr. Behrens and Mr. Hadley?

A. Yes. I'm sorry, Mr. Behrens and Mr. Hadley.

Q. Where are the other two?

A. I don't really know. I kind of lost track of them after they left us.

Q. Do you know what happened to the prototype levels?

A. No I don't really know. I think one of them was exchanged for the commercial models made by Bullivant, model B-150A, after they came on the market. But I don't really know and I don't know what happened to the other ones.

Q. No further questions.

THE VIDOGRAPHER: This ends Tape Number 1 and concludes the testimony of Charley A. Cooley in the matter of Bullivant Tool versus Pacific Machine Corporation.

The date is August 16, 2005, the time is 10:30:02. Off the record.

(Deposition adjourned at 10:30 a.m.)

(Signature waived.)

CERTIFICATE OF COURT REPORTER

UNITED STATES OF AMERICA)

STATE OF WASHINGTON)

I, Kathy Geyne Kessling, the reporter before whom the foregoing deposition was taken, do hereby certify that the witness whose testimony appears in the foregoing deposition was sworn by me; that the testimony of said witness was taken by me in machine shorthand and thereafter transcribed by computer-aided transcription; that said deposition is a true record of the testimony given by said witness; that I am neither counsel for, related to, nor employed by any of the parties to the action in which this deposition was taken; and, further, that I am not a relative or employee of any attorney or counsel employed by the parties hereto, or financial or otherwise interested in the outcome of this action.

KATHY GEYNE KESSLING

Notary Public in and for the

State of Washington

My Commission Expires August 5, 2006.

Page 22

Kessling Deposition Services
206-555-1234

Witness Name: Charley A. Cooley
Volume:
Re: Bullivant Tools v.
Pacific Machine Corporation

Deposition Date: August 16, 2005
Court Reporter: Kathy Geyne Kessling
Case No. 04-9876

Page	Line	Correction
11	22	"rungs" should be "runs"

I hereby certify that I have read the foregoing deposition, and that this deposition, together with any corrections, is a true and accurate record of my testimony given at this deposition.

Charles A. Cooley
Witness's Signature

Subscribed and sworn to before me this _______day

of ________________, 20______.

Notary Public:
My Commission Expires:

SECTION G-2

IN THE UNITED STATES DISTRICT COURT FOR WASHINGTON

WESTERN DISTRICT

Bullivant Tool, Inc.,)

Plaintiff,) Case No. 04 9876

v.)

Pacific Machine Corporation)

Defendant.)

VIDEOTAPED DEPOSITION OF GLEN E. EAKIN

Friday, June 10, 2005

Reported by: Kathy G. Kessling, RPR

Page 1

Kessling Deposition Services
206-555-1234

The videotaped deposition of Glen E. Eakin, a witness herein, was convened on June 10, 2005, commencing at 9:08 a.m., at the offices of Flotsam & Jetsam, 98765 Ocean Avenue, Seattle, Washington, 98120, before Kathy Geyne Kessling, Registered Professional Reporter.

APPEARANCES

For Plaintiff:

MR. AMOS A. ADAMS, Esquire
1000 Japan Trade Building
Seattle, Washington 98120
Telephone: 206-354-2400

For Defendant:

CHARLES F. JETSAM, Esquire
Flotsam & Jetsam
98765 Ocean Avenue
Seattle, Washington 98120
Telephone: 206-354-2800

Also present: T.J. Sullivan, Videographer

Page 3

Kessling Deposition Services
206-555-1234

CONTENTS

EXHIBITS

(Exhibits retained by counsel.)

PROCEEDINGS

THE VIDEOGRAPHER: On the record with Tape Number 1 of the videotape deposition of Glen E. Eakin, taken by the Plaintiff in the matter of Bullivant Tool, Inc., versus Pacific Machine Corporation in the United States District Court for Washington, Eastern District, Case Number 04 9876.

This Deposition is being held at the law offices of Flotsam & Jetsam, 98765 Ocean Avenue, Seattle, Washington, 98120, on June 10, 2005, at approximately 9:08 a.m.

My name is T.J. Sullivan, representing Kessling Deposition Services. I'm a certified legal video specialist.

The court reporter is Kathy Geyne Kessling representing Kessling Deposition Services. I'm a certified court reporter.

Will counsel please introduce themselves and indicate which parties they represent.

MR. JETSAM: I am Charles F. Jetsam, counsel for Pacific Machine Corporation.

MR. ADAMS: And I am Mr. Adams, and I represent Bullivant Tool, Inc.

GLEN E. EAKIN,

called for examination, having been first duly sworn, was examined and testified as follows;

EXAMINATION BY COUNSEL FOR BULLIVANT TOOL CORPORATION BY Mr. Adams.

Q. Mr. Eakin as you know my name is Amos Adams and I am your attorney in this case. I will be taking your deposition today. Can you tell me your job?

A. I am the vice President of Bullivant Tool, Inc.

Q. Where is Bullivant Tool located?

A. 135 N. LaSalle, Chicago, Illinois 60603

Q. It's the plaintiff in this case?

A. Yes it is.

Q. Mr. Eakin, are you on any medications that might impact your concentration or stamina?

A. Yes I am.

Q. Can you describe them please?

A. I recently had open heart surgery and am prone to tire very easily. I taken a blood thinner and it exacerbates the problem. It also keeps my blood pressure low which tends to fatigue me even more. So I suppose if this goes on a long time I might need to take more breaks than you folks might otherwise take, if that's all right with you.

Q. No problem. I don't think this will take long in any event. We simply want to get your testimony down in writing in case you can't make the trial.

A. Thank you.
Q. Mr. Eakin when were you born?
A. I was born on April 18, 1954.
Q. Can you tell me a little bit about your education?
A. I graduated from Eastern Illinois State College in May 1982.
Q. What did you study?
A. I studied Business Administration. My major area of focus was sales and marketing.
Q. Did you receive a degree?
A. I received a Bachelor of Arts in Business Administration.
Q. What did you do upon graduation?
A. Right after graduation I joined the sales department of Bullivant Tool, Inc. I've spent my entire career at Bullivant.
Q. What was your job at the time you joined?
A. I was a sales engineer, what they call a "sales engineer." Basically I was a salesman for our tools.
Q. Can you simply describe your career at Bullivant.
A. Sure. I worked in the field in sales for a number of years, and in 1986 I was promoted to Mid-Eastern Sales Manager. In that job I had some supervisory responsibility over all

of the salesman at in the mid-state regions. I began to have some interface at that time with the marketing people and product development folks. Basically if we had ideas from the field that we thought could be developed into products we communicated them back to the main office.

In 1991 I was appointed the General Sales Manager. In that job I had responsibility over all of the salesmen and the regional sales managers.

Q. When was that?

A. In 1991. I don't remember exactly when.

Q. Did your duties change?

A. Well they expanded more than changed. Like I said, I had responsibility for all of the salesmen rather than those in just the region and as General Sales Manager I also had responsibility for the Regional Sales Managers. In addition my interfacing with the marketing and research & development folks increased because I was back at headquarters more often.

Q. What happened next?

A. In 1998 I was appointed Vice-President of Sales and Marketing. That's the position I currently hold.

Q. How did your duties change if at all?

A. Basically I picked up responsibility for marketing and I acquired a new person to do the day-to-day handling of sales, the new General Sales Manager.

Q. Mr. Eakin, are you familiar generally with the subject matter of this lawsuit?

A. Yes of course. It's a patent lawsuit on the patent we acquired concerning the adjustable level.

Q. I'd like to ask you some questions about the patent and your acquisition of it. I'm showing you what has been marked as Plaintiff's Exhibit 2. Do you recognize this?

A. Yes, it's a letter of September 2, 1996 from Mr. Parrish to us.

Q. By us who do you mean?

A. Bullivant. It was sent to Bullivant Tool Company. It was an unsolicited letter from one of our customers to us about the patent involved in this lawsuit.

Q. When you say it was sent to you by one of your customers what do you mean by that?

A. It was sent to us by George Parrish, and he was founder or President or something like that of the Parrish Construction Company in Columbus, Ohio. They used our tools, and so I called him a customer.

Q. Before I move on can you tell me a little bit about Bullivant Tool, Inc.?

A. Sure, we are one of the premier tool companies in the

industry. We cater primarily to professional contractors because our grade of tool is higher than what you might find in the local hardware store. We design and create specialized tools for specialized jobs as well as more general tools. You can find our brand on virtually every quality construction site. In recent years we have branched out to include a lower grade model of tools for higher grade consumer stores, but we don't really compete at the very low end of the market.

Q. Going back to Plaintiff's Exhibit 2 do you recall seeing this before?

A. Sure. This came to me when it was sent to the company.

Q. Do you have an understanding of why it came to you, given that it's not addressed to you?

A. Yes. As I told you I was in charge of marketing at the time. That was one of the departments under me. Since this concerned what Mr. Parrish said was a new type of level it came to me to evaluate whether we would want to get into that business.

Q. What was your thinking about it?

A. Well at the time we already had an extendable level but Mr. Parrish said that his was an improvement. He also pointed out, as you see here, that he had a patent application on the level that had been approved in the Patent Office. We had a patent on our earlier level so I knew a little bit about patents.

Q. When you say you had a patent on your earlier level what do you mean?

A. One of our owners, Mr. Bullivant, had a U.S. patent. It was on the level that extended but it didn't have any kind of lock on it.

Q. How did you know about that patent?

A. Well, I was in sales for quite a period of time. We always referred to it as the patented extension level and hyped it in our sales calls and promotional meetings.

Q. I'm showing you what is marked as Defendant's Exhibit 1, do you recognize this?

A. Yes. This is the patent I was referring to. Let's see it was granted on April 30, 1991. That's about the time I was moving from the field to the General Sales Manager position, and I remember we would use the fact that the level was patented as part of our marketing and sales efforts.

Q. What specifically did you do on receiving the letter from Mr. Parrish, Plaintiff's Exhibit 2?

A. Well, I told my boss about it and said I thought we should follow-up.

Page 11

Kessling Deposition Services
206-555-1234

Q. Who was your boss?
A. Dave Horton.
Q. And what was his title?
A. He was President of the company.
Q. I'm showing you what I've marked as Plaintiff's Exhibit 3. It's an e-mail dated September 23, 1996. Do you recognize that?
(Plaintiff's Exhibit No. 3 marked for identification.)
A. Yes.
Q. What is it?
A. Well, like you said, it's an e-mail I wrote to Dave Horton telling him about the inquiry from Mr. Parrish.
Q. Did you write this e-mail on or about the date indicated?
A. Sure. This came from our files.
Q. Did you have a response to this e-mail?
A. Yes I did.
Q. What was the response?
A. Well, Dave stuck his head in my office and told me to go for it.
Q. Did he give you any more specific instructions?
A. No. I think he just wanted me to run with the ball.

Page 12

At this time I was still General Sales Manager, and I think he was giving me an opportunity to strut my stuff and see if I could handle something that had a little marketing aspect to it.

Q. What did you do?

A. Well, I called Mr. Parrish and told him I'd like to chat with him about his letter.

Q. What happened next?

A. We had several telephone conversations, including one with his partner, Mr. Cooley. Basically a good deal of our discussion before we got together was to see if each of us was serious and to set up a time and date when we could meet.

Q. When you say to see if you were serious what do you mean?

A. I got the impression they wanted to see if we really would make this kind of tool, and we wanted to find out if they had unrealistic money demands. As I said, we make high end tools which means they tend to be a little bit expensive, although we think they're a great value. But we're not mass-market merchandisers. We're a small but respected quality tool maker and I think they wanted to find out whether we would be interested in making their kind of level.

Q. You mentioned royalty demands. What were you interested in learning?

Page 13

Kessling Deposition Services
206-555-1234

A. Well, we wanted to learn whether they had unduly optimistic expectations about how much money they would make. When I asked them about this on the telephone they said that we would probably know better than they of what kind of royalties were appropriate in the industry.

Q. What was your reaction to that?

A. I was very surprised. While they're right that we probably knew more than they did, most small inventors when they bring an idea to us tend to ask for the sky and not realize that royalty rates can't make a product unprofitable.

Q. What happened next?

A. We had them in to our offices in Chicago during the Trade Show and hammered out a deal.

Q. How long did it take?

A. It took no time at all. Less than a day. Most of the time was spent talking about the business, the construction business.

Q. Where did the meeting take place?

A. The meeting took place at our patent attorneys in Chicago, in their offices. We figured if we were going to reach a deal we could have the assignment drawn up right then and there. We brought them over to our offices as well just to give them a tour.

Q. Can you describe the negotiations?

A. Well we told them we'd be interested in making the tool and royalty rates in the business range from 3 to 7 percent of the wholesale price of the tool. Recognizing that there were two inventors, that would generally mean one and one-half to 3 and one-half percent each. However, we said this was a really nifty little device, and we did not think the sales volumes would be extraordinarily high, so we said we would offer them each five percent of the wholesale price.

Q. What was their reaction?

A. They said yes. They said they wanted to see the product in the marketplace and thought we were the company to do it.

Q. What did you do next?

A. That's when we told them we'd have a lawyers draft up an assignment and we would go tour the Bullivant offices down the street. We said we'd come back and sign it and that would be it.

Q. Is that what happened?

A. Not quite. While we were still chatting in our offices a courier brought the assignment over and we signed it in our offices.

Q. I'm showing you what has been marked as Plaintiff's

Exhibit 4. It is a document bearing the title of Assignment. Do you recognize this document?

A. Yes.

Q. What is it?

A. That's the assignment our lawyers drafted and that we had signed.

Q. I note that the notary date is March 20, 1997. Is that the day you had the negotiations?

A. Yes. The National Hardware Show was in Chicago on that day, and that's the day we met with Mr. Parrish and Mr. Cooley.

Q. Did you see them sign this document?

A. Sure. I offered them a glass of scotch to celebrate, but they declined. It was all very friendly. They signed it in our office, we had it notarized by a notary, I made a copy for them, and we shook hands. I took them in to see Dave Horton, too.

Q. Did you offer this new product for sale, the one described in the patent to Mr. Parrish and Mr. Cooley?

A. Yes. It was basically a replacement for our B-100 extensible level.

Q. What was this new product called?

A. It was the B-150, and quickly became known as the B-

150A.

Q. What was the difference between the B-150 and the B-150A.

A. No real difference, really. It had to do with the finish on some of the materials which made it easier to extend or slide. They were basically the same design but different details, making the B-150A a slight improvement over the B-150.

Q. How were sales?

A. Initially sales were great. We came out with the product in late `97 and sales through `97 and `98 were outstanding.

Q. You say they were initially great. Did sales continue in that vein?

A. No, there was a construction slump in 1999, really an overall economic slump, and that caused a slow down in the building trades.

Q. Have sales picked up as the economy has recovered?

A. No they haven't.

Q. Is there still a slow down in the building trades?

A. No, construction has gone up again. In fact new housing starts are great as interest rates have been kept low, particularly mortgage interest rates.

Q. Have sales of the Bullivant B-150A gone up as the

building trades have improved their economic condition?

A. No, on the contrary, our sales of that level have been terrible. Our other tools are doing well but we've been doing terribly with the B-150A.

Q. Do you have any explanation for that?

MR. JETSAM: Objection, calls for speculation.

Q. Mr. Eakin, as Vice President of Sales and Marketing with responsibility for all marketing and sales activities of the Plaintiff, do you have any understanding as to why your sales of B-150A have remained depressed even though your other tool sales have increased.

A. Yes I do.

Q. Can you share it with us.

MR. JETSAM: Same objection. Witness has answered.

A. Yes. I think it's attributable to the infringement of our patent.

Q. You say infringement of your patent. What do you mean by that?

MR. JETSAM: Objection. Calls for expert testimony. Can I have a continuing objection on this?

MR. ADAMS: Yes sure.

A. I mean the fact that PMC is making the same thing and undercutting us in the marketplace.

Q. You say PMC, do you mean Pacific Machine Corporation?
A. Yes.
Q. When did you first hear about PMC offering a similar level?
A. I discovered it myself. I was on vacation in Jellystone National Park when I discovered it. Funny how work intrudes on your vacations.
Q. When was this?
A. It was in the summer of 1999.
Q. Can you describe the circumstances?
A. Yes. As I said, we were vacationing at Jellystone and I had occasion to go into a hardware store, one of the upscale hardware stores in the area. I tend to do that even while I'm on vacation. While there I saw an extendable level that looked astonishingly like ours.
Q. What level was that?
A. The level was the PMC-20.
Q. What did you do when you saw that?
A. I asked the man behind the counter who made it and he told me Pacific Machine Corporation.
Q. Had you ever heard of Pacific Machine Corporation?
A. No. I figured it was a West coast operation, so I asked him where it was. He told me in Washington State, so I

had someone look it up and they found out it was in Renton, Washington.

Q. Who looked it up for you?

A. I don't know. Someone in the office. It wasn't as easy even in 1999 to just pop on the internet and do a Google search to find these companies. Someone else did it for me, but it was PMC.

Q. What did you do next?

A. I bought it. I bought it from the hardware store and brought it back to work to show to Mr. Horton.

Q. I'm going to show you an e-mail dated August 21, 1999. Do you recognize that?

A. Yes. It's an e-mail I wrote to Dave telling him about the PMC-20. I wrote it right when I got home. I didn't even wait to go into the office. I remember being so incensed about the PMC-20 because, of course, I had been involved in the negotiations for the patent so I was very sensitive to the issue.

Q. By the time you wrote your e-mail, Plaintiff's Exhibit 5, had you known where PMC was located?

A. I don't think so. I knew it was in Washington from the sales clerk, but don't think I had anybody look it up yet.

Q. Your e-mail says that the PMC-20 level "is similar to"

your Model B-150A. Do you see that?

A. Yes I do.

Q. What did you mean by that?

MR. JETSAM: Objection, calls for a legal conclusion.

MR. ADAMS: I'm simply asking him factually what he meant. You can answer.

A. Well, it's pretty self-evident. I looked at the level from Pacific Machine Corporation and it looked very similar in my mind and in my eye to our own model B150-A. As I say in the e-mail, I would show him the actual level when I got into work. I simply wanted to alert him to the situation because we are going to have to make some decisions.

Q. What happened next?

A. Well, we discussed it and agreed that we should write a letter to PMC. We decided that the letter should come from Mr. Horton as President and should send a copy of the patent.

Q. Did you do that?

A. I'm showing you what's been marked as Plaintiff's Exhibit 6. It's a letter on Bullivant letterhead dated September 27, 1999, to Mr. Millard C. Pringle, President of PMC.

(Plaintiff's Exhibit No. 6
marked for identification.)

A. Yes, this is the letter we sent.

Q. What was your purpose in writing this letter?

MR. JETSAM: Lack of foundation.

Q. Let me rephrase the question. Let me strike it in fact. Did you have any role in preparing Plaintiff's Exhibit 6?

A. Yes. I wrote it.

Q. Did Mr. Horton make any changes to what you wrote?

A. No.

Q. Who selected the language to be used in the letter?

A. I did. I wrote it.

Q. What was your purpose in preparing that letter?

A. Well we discussed bringing PMC's attention to our patent, so we wanted them to have a copy of the patent and be able to compare it to their PMC-20. Then we wanted to ask them to cease selling that product.

Q. I note that the letter says that you wanted them to "immediately cease" marketing the PMC-20 and all similar levels "in the absence of a license from us." What did you intend to convey by discussing a license?

A. We didn't want to be too harsh. We wanted them to understand that we were paying a license and that if they were going to sell a product like ours they would have to pay a commission or a royalty. It seemed only fair if we were paying and we took the risk in bringing it out that they should pay at least what we were and a little extra for us. Essentially I was inviting them to ask us how much it would cost to allow them to continue selling at least their existing inventory.

Q. What do you mean by existing inventory?

A. We really wanted market exclusivity. We were willing to be reasonable and allow them to sell the products they had already manufactured, assuming it wasn't too many. The product didn't look like a cheap knock-off so we didn't think they had a large number on hand and we were willing to be reasonable and discuss allowing them to sell them off. We really did not want to enter into a license that would allow them to continue to manufacture the product, however, we did not want to be too harsh.

Q. I note that the letter continues with the indication that you were going to bring the matter to the attention of your attorneys. Do you see that?

A. Yes I do.

Q. Did you do so?

A. Yes. We forwarded a copy of this letter to our patent attorneys.

Q. In other words you forwarded it to me.

A. Yes, I did.

Q. You indicated that PMC should "expect to hear from

them shortly." Do you see that?

A. Yes.

Q. What did you mean by that?

A. Just what it said. I wanted them to get back to me either with an indication they would stop selling the product or a request that we negotiate a license, at least for a sell-off period. I wanted them to recognize that we were serious and that if they didn't get back to us they would hear from our lawyers.

Q. Did you ever hear back from them?

A. No I didn't. There was nothing but stone cold silence.

Q. Did you follow-up with them at that time?

A. No I didn't.

Q. Did you have your lawyers follow-up with them?

A. No.

Q. Why not.

A. Well a couple of reasons really. As I mentioned right at that time there was an economic downturn in the economy. We were not selling our B150-A or any other tools at that time and so revenue was a bit tight. A lawsuit would have meant even more financial hardship, at least for us. It just didn't seem like a good time to be spending money on lawyers.

Q. Was there anything else?

A. Yes. In November 1999, in part because of the downturn in the economy, we signed a Merger Option Agreement with another company.

Q. What did that have to do with whether you followed-up or not?

A. There was a provision in the agreement, the Merger Option Agreement that prevented either company from taking any action as a Plaintiff in any civil litigation without the consent of the other party.

Q. Why was that?

A. We didn't want either company to be starting an expensive civil litigation and then going into the merger without the other party at least understanding what it was getting into.

Q. Did you discuss the possibility of bringing a patent infringement action with this other company?

A. Yes we did.

Q. What was the outcome of those discussions?

A. They thought it would not be advisable and they declined to consent to go forward with a lawsuit.

Q. Did they give a reason?

A. Only in general terms. Of course, we hadn't mergered

and therefore it was a bit of an arm's length activity. But they said that patent litigation was terribly expensive and they did not want to go forward with it or give their consent to it.

Q. What was your reaction?

A. Well, we had no choice. But I guess I figured that they had a reason for saying patent litigation was terribly expensive. I didn't know it at the time, but it sure has turned out to be true. Is this a good time for a break? I sure could use a few minutes.

Q. Sure. Let's go off the record for a few minutes.

COURT REPORTER: GOING OFF THE RECORD.

COURT REPORTER: GOING BACK ON THE RECORD.

Q. Mr. Eakin, can you tell us who this other company with which you signed the Merger Option Agreement.

A. No I really can't.

Q. Why not?

A. We have a confidentiality requirement with them.

Q. What type of confidentiality requirement?

A. We're not allowed to identify the name of the other company under any circumstances unless, I guess, if we are ordered to do so by a Court. But we've agreed not to identify each other and we've agreed that the obligation continues whether or not the merger took place.

Q. Did the merger take place?

A. No. Ultimately, due to a number of circumstances, neither party exercised the merger option.

Q. Is there still an opportunity for that to take place?

A. No.

Q. When did that opportunity end?

A. The merger option expired on April 19, 2002.

Q. Since that time have you revealed the identity of the other company to any one?

A. No. We've kept our part of the bargain. And so have they.

Q. You anticipated my next question. I have no further questions.

CROSS EXAMINATION BY MR. JETSAM.

Q. Mr. Eakin, what was the name of the other company with whom you had a Merger Option Agreement?

A. I told you, I can't reveal it. We have a confidentiality requirement.

Q. I understand what you told me, but I'm entitled to know the name of the company. You brought it up so please tell me the name of the other company.

A. No.

MR. ADAMS: Objection. He's already explained that he

can't do so.

Q. I'm not really interested in what agreements you made or didn't make, I'm interested in discovering information that might help me defend my client. Now you said one of the reasons you did not follow-up with PMC, even so far as to write a letter, was because of some merger option agreement with some unidentified company. You raised the point. Tell me the name of the other company.

MR. ADAMS: Objection.

A. No. I won't.

Q. Do you have a copy of the Merger Option Agreement?

A. Yes I do.

Q. Where?

A. In my briefcase.

Q. When did you last look at it.

A. I looked at it today.

Q. For what purpose?

A. To get the date, the date the option expired. I wasn't exactly sure of the date.

Q. So you looked at it in order to refresh your recollection in preparing to testify today?

A. Yes I did.

Q. Then give it to me.

MR. ADAMS: Objection. He's already told you it's confidential.

A. No I won't give it to you. I thought we just explained this.

Q. I don't care whether it's confidential or not. We have a Protective Order in this case and I'll continue to keep it confidential but I'm entitled to look at it. You reviewed that document for purposes of refreshing your recollection to testify under oath today. I am entitled until the rules to the document so give it to me.

A. No.

MR. ADAMS: Counsel, we can work this out.

MR. JETSAM: We can work it out when you give it to me. I'm entitled to examine the document this witness looked at today to assist his testimony.

A. Sir, the Merger Option Agreement requires that all this material remain confidential. It even says I can't disclose this document, the merger option document. It's really not that mysterious, I just can't do it without breaking the agreement.

Q. Do you have the document here in the room?

A. Yes it's in my briefcase.

Q. Have you shown it to your lawyer.

Page 29

Kessling Deposition Services
206-555-1234

A. No.
Q. Have you discussed it with your lawyer?
MR. ADAMS: Objection, privileged.
MR. JETSAM: Counsel, I just want to know why this document which I'm entitled to is being withheld.
MR. ADAMS: Well, that wasn't your question. Your question was objectionable, and the reason the document is being withheld has already been explained to you several times. Counsel will agree, if you wish, to make the Merger Option Agreement available to the Court for *in camera* inspection. I make this offer without ever having seen it myself.
MR. EAKIN: What is *in camera* inspection?
MR. JETSAM: Don't worry. It's given to the Court and the Court looks at it without telling anybody about it and then decides whether it needs to be produced. If the Court orders it produced you can produce it without worry because it was a Court Order. If the Court says it has nothing to do with this case they'll give it back to me and I'll give it to you and that will be the end of it. Does that seem reasonable.
MR. ADAMS: Yes it does. We'll agree to that.
Q. Mr. Eakin does the Merger Option Agreement prevent you from writing a follow-up letter to PMC to follow-up on your communications in Plaintiff's Exhibit 6.

A. I'm not sure I know what you mean?

Q. You said that it prevented you from bringing the civil action. Did it prevent your company from writing letters?

A. No.

Q. Did it prevent you from telling PMC you hadn't heard back from them?

A. No.

Q. Did it prevent you from trying to see whether PMC would be interested in a license?

A. No.

Q. Did it prevent you from entering into a license with PMC?

A. No.

Q. Did it prevent you from asking PMC again to stop marketing the PMC-20.

A. No. It only prevented our filing of a lawsuit, like I said.

Q. So there was nothing that prevented you from taking the time it takes to write a three paragraph letter and the cost of a first class mail stamp to notify PMC that you wanted an answer to the in Plaintiff's Exhibit 6.

MR. ADAMS: Counsel you're beginning to harass the witness.

MR. JETSAM: You can answer the question.

A. No, I guess it didn't.

Q. Now you indicated that in November of 1999 you signed this Merger Option Agreement that you won't produce to us. That wasn't your first inquiry with this unnamed company was it?

A. Inquiry?

Q. That wasn't the first time you ever contacted them about a possible merger was it?

A. No.

Q. Conversations between your two companies had been going on for some time isn't that correct?

A. I suppose they had.

Q. In fact, conversations between your two companies had been going on for several months at least.

A. I suppose you're right, but really the first contacts were with Dave Horton our President.

Q. So at the time you wrote Plaintiff's Exhibit 6 and it was sent by Mr. Horton you'd already had these conversations started with this other unnamed company isn't that correct?

A. You may be right. I just don't know for sure.

Q. So you had already told PMC that they should expect to hear from your attorneys before you made the agreement with this unnamed company that you wouldn't bring civil action without their permission.

A. Sure that's right.

Q. And you made this statement to PMC in Plaintiff's Exhibit 6 even though you had already begun to have discussions with this other unnamed company. Isn't that right?

A. Again, that may be right but I'm not 100% certain. I don't know exactly remember when the conversation about merger started.

Q. You testify about a downturn in the economy generally and the building trade specifically. None of the loss of sales that you were experiencing in 1999 could be attributed to the activity of PMC, isn't that correct?

A. 1999?

Q. Yes.

A. You're probably right.

Q. No loss of sales in 1999 can be attributed to the PMC-20's sale by PMC, correct?

A. Yes.

Q. And at the time you first saw the PMC-20 you had never heard of Pacific Machine Corporation. Isn't that correct?

A. Yes, that's correct.

Q. And yet you still wrote a letter threatening PMC with a lawsuit.

Q. Well I don't . . .

MR. ADAMS: Objection. Mischaracterizes the record.

A. Well I don't know that we threatened them with a lawsuit. Like I said, we didn't want to be to harsh but we didn't want to let the matter slide.

Q. Yet that's just what you did, let the matter slide, isn't that correct?

A. No, not really.

Q. Well you did nothing after sending the letter, Plaintiff's Exhibit 6, until you filed this lawsuit, isn't that correct?

A. Yes.

Q. So you did nothing in 1999, correct?

A. Well nothing further, we had this agreement . . .

Q. Just answer the question. You did nothing further in 1999 other than write your threatening letter, isn't that correct?

A. Yes.

Q. And in 2000 you did nothing.

A. Pursuant to our agreement in the Merger Option Agreement which prohibited us from filing suit we did nothing.

Q. Mr. Eakin, you just referenced the Merger Option Agreement which you won't give to me. Yet you agree that Merger Option Agreement did not prohibit you from writing a letter to

PMC did it?

A. No it did not.

Q. And you did not write a letter in 2000 did you, to PMC?

A. No.

Q. And you did not write a letter in 2001?

A. No.

Q. And you did not write a letter in early 2002 did you?

A. No.

Q. And on April 19, 2002, when your Merger Option Agreement expired and you could even bring a lawsuit you did not do so did you?

A. Did not do what?

Q. You did not file a lawsuit against PMC.

A. No.

Q. And you did not write a letter to PMC?

A. No.

Q. And you did not write a letter in 2003?

A. No.

Q. And you did not write a letter in 2004?

A. We filed suit.

Q. Exactly, the next thing you did after writing Plaintiff's Exhibit 6 was file the Complaint in this lawsuit on

Page 35

Kessling Deposition Services
206-555-1234

April 20, 2004, isn't that right?

A. Yes.

Q. No further questions.

REDIRECT EXAMINATION BY MR. ADAMS.

Q. Mr. Eakin on cross examination you indicated that in 1999 no loss of sales could be attributed to the activity of PMC, do you recall that?

A. Yes.

Q. What about 2000?

A. Well things were beginning to pick up in 2000 but our B-150A sales did not pick up as much so I think the infringement had something to do with it.

Q. What about 2001?

A. Clearly we were experiencing loss of sales to the PMC-20 in 2001.

Q. How about 2002?

A. Same thing. It was getting worse.

Q. How about in 2003?

A. It really got bad in 2003. In fact, we've had severe losses in sales during the nine months before we brought the lawsuit.

Q. No further questions.

(Deposition adjourned at 1:12 p.m.)

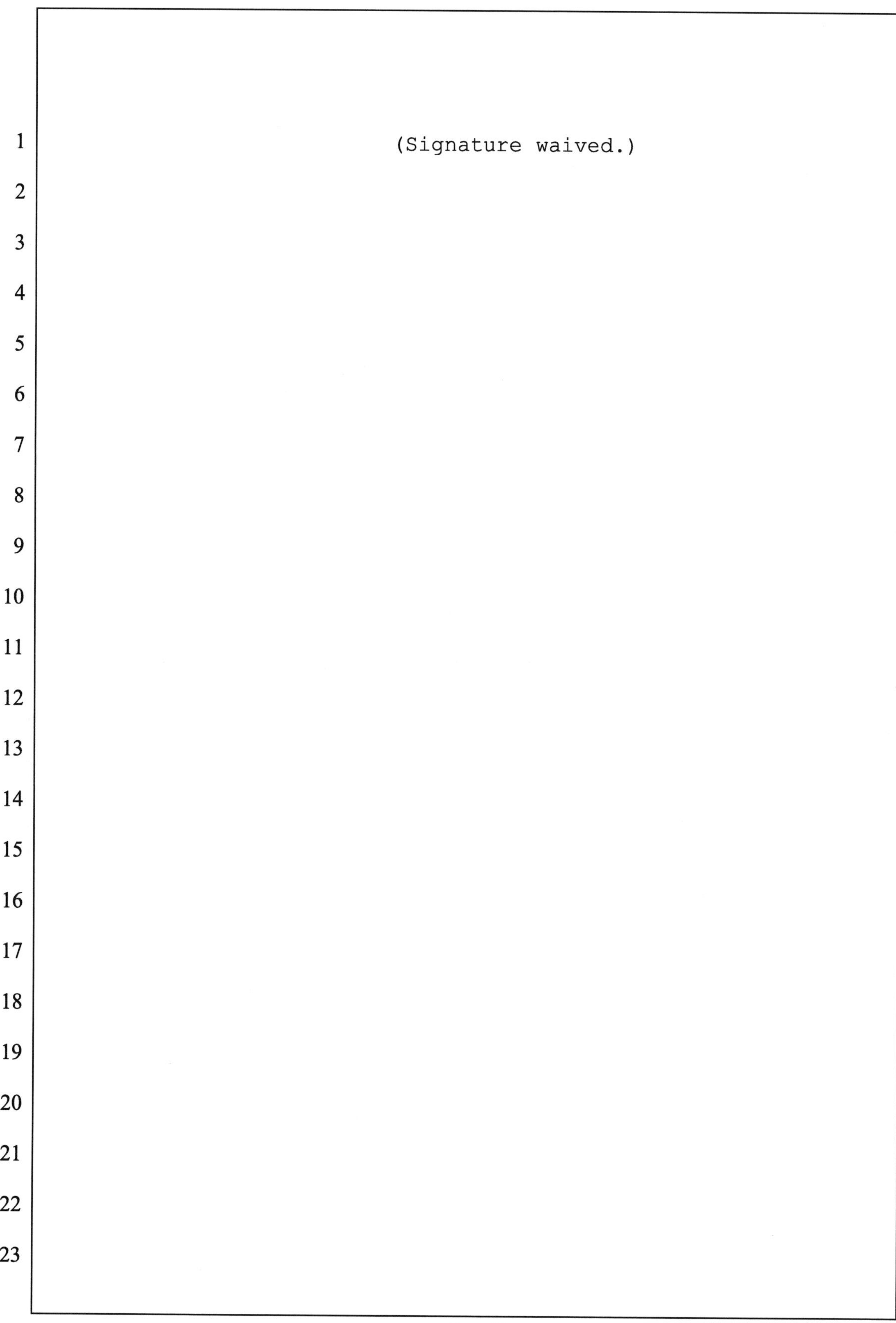
(Signature waived.)

Page 37

Kessling Deposition Services
206-555-1234

CERTIFICATE OF COURT REPORTER

UNITED STATES OF AMERICA)

STATE OF WASHINGTON)

I, Kathy Geyne Kessling, the reporter before whom the foregoing deposition was taken, do hereby certify that the witness whose testimony appears in the foregoing deposition was sworn by me; that the testimony of said witness was taken by me in machine shorthand and thereafter transcribed by computer-aided transcription; that said deposition is a true record of the testimony given by said witness; that I am neither counsel for, related to, nor employed by any of the parties to the action in which this deposition was taken; and, further, that I am not a relative or employee of any attorney or counsel employed by the parties hereto, or financial or otherwise interested in the outcome of this action.

KATHY GEYNE KESSLING

Notary Public in and for the

State of Washington

My Commission Expires August 5, 2006

Witness Name: Glen E. Eakin
Volume:
Re: Bullivant Tools v.
Pacific Machine Corporation

Deposition Date: June 10, 2005
Court Reporter: Kathy Geyne Kessling
Case No. 04-9876

Page	Line	Correction

I hereby certify that I have read the foregoing deposition, and that this deposition, together with any corrections, is a true and accurate record of my testimony given at this deposition.

____
Witness's Signature

Subscribed and sworn to before me this _______day

of __________________, 20______.

____
Notary Public:
My Commission Expires:

SECTION G-3

IN THE UNITED STATES DISTRICT COURT FOR WASHINGTON

WESTERN DISTRICT

Bullivant Tool, Inc.,)

Plaintiff,) Case No. 04 9876

v.)

Pacific Machine Corporation)

Defendant.)

VIDEOTAPED DEPOSITION OF ALAN C. EDGAR

Wednesday, June 8, 2005

Reported by: Kathy G. Kessling, RPR

The videotaped deposition of Alan C. Edgar, a witness herein, was convened on June 8, 2005, commencing at 9:08 a.m., at the offices of Flotsam & Jetsam, 98765 Ocean Avenue, Seattle, Washington, 98120, before Kathy Geyne Kessling, Registered Professional Reporter.

Page 2

Kessling Deposition Services
206-555-1234

SECTION G

APPEARANCES

For Plaintiff:
MR. AMOS A. ADAMS, Esquire
1000 Japan Trade Building
Seattle, Washington 98120
Telephone: 206-354-2400

For Defendant:
CHARLES F. JETSAM, Esquire
Flotsam & Jetsam
98765 Ocean Avenue
Seattle, Washington 98120
Telephone: 206-354-2800

Also present: T.J. Sullivan, Videographer

CONTENTS

EXHIBITS

(Exhibits retained by counsel.)

SECTION G

PROCEEDINGS

THE VIDEOGRAPHER: On the record with Tape Number 1 of the videotape deposition of Alan C. Edgar, taken by the Defendant in the matter of Bullivant Tool, Inc., versus Pacific Machine Corporation in the United States District Court for Washington, Eastern District, Case Number 04 9876.

This Deposition is being held at the law offices of Flotsam & Jetsam, 98765 Ocean Avenue, Seattle, Washington, 98120, on June 8, 2005, at approximately 9:08 a.m.

My name is T.J. Sullivan, representing Kessling Deposition Services. I'm a certified legal video specialist.

The court reporter is Kathy Geyne Kessling representing Kessling Deposition Services. I'm a certified court reporter.

Will counsel please introduce themselves and indicate which parties they represent.

MR. JETSAM: I am Charles F. Jetsam, counsel for Pacific Machine Corporation.

MR. ADAMS: And I am Mr. Adams, and I represent Bullivant Tool, Inc.

ALAN C. EDGAR,

called for examination, having been first duly sworn, was examined and testified as follows;

EXAMINATION BY COUNSEL FOR BULLIVANT TOOL CORPORATION BY Mr. Adams.

Q. Mr. Edgar, my name is Mr. Adams and I'll be taking this deposition. Have you ever been deposed before?

A. Yes.

Q. So you know the rules I take it. Simply answer the questions I give to you audibly, without shaking your head yes or no because the Court Reporter can't take it down.

A. Yes, I think so.

Q. If you don't understand a question please let me know because if you answer it we will assume you understand it.

A. Yes I understand that.

Q. Okay. What kind of case were you deposed in?

A. It was a traffic accident case. I observed a traffic accident and was what I think you call a third party witness.

Q. Okay Mr. Edgar, for the record can you tell us when you were born?

A. I was born October 18, 1968.

Q. Can you give us a little background about your education.

A. Including high school?

Q. No, let's take it since high school.

A. Yes sir, I obtained a bachelor's degree in mechanical

engineering from the University of California at Berkeley.

Q. Anything else?

A. No.

Q. When did you receive your mechanical engineering degree?

A. In 1990.

Q. What did you do after that?

A. I went to work.

Q. For whom?

A. Boeing Aircraft Corporation.

Q. Where?

A. In Seattle, Washington.

Q. What did you do at Boeing?

A. My title was Engineer-Aircraft Systems.

Q. What were your duties?

A. I worked on the design of various mechanical systems used in aircraft.

Q. What type of systems?

A. I wasn't quite finished. In addition, I worked on mechanical systems involved in the manufacture and fabrication of aircraft.

Q. Okay, are you done?

A. Yes.

Q. What kinds of aircraft systems did you work on?
A. Brakes, plumbing, passenger seat securement, windows, galley mechanics, and others. There are so many I cannot recall them all.
Q. What kind of installation issues did you deal with?
A. Anything involved in the manufacture of an aircraft.
Q. Can you be more specific?
A. No.
Q. Can you give me some examples?
A. Yes.
Q. Would you do so?
A. Sure. I fabricated, or designed, tooling for the mechanics to use in installing and refurbishing the passenger compartments of aircraft. At one time we had aircraft that did not have the little safety lights on the floor that would guide you to an exit in the case of a power loss. I helped design the tools used to install those lights, for example. I helped design the parts for aircraft lavatories so that the installation during manufacture would be easier. I helped modify the tooling used by the ground crew in opening the baggage stowage compartments. All kinds of mechanical things on aircraft. These are just examples.
Q. How long did you work for Boeing?

A. I never added it up. I left Boeing in March 1995 so that would be about five years.

Q. Who did you go to work for?

A. Pacific Machine Corporation.

Q. What was your job?

A. To develop new products.

Q. What was your title?

A. Development Engineer.

Q. Other than developing new products did you have any other duties?

A. Yes.

Q. What were they?

A. Basically, to do anything from an engineering standpoint that needed to be done.

Q. What did you spend most of your time on?

A. Developing new products.

Q. Why were you hired to development new products?

MR. JETSAM: Objection, calls for speculation.

A. I can only guess, but I suppose it was because the company wanted to develop new products.

Q. Were you told why you were hired?

A. Yes.

Q. What were you told?

A. I was told the company wanted to develop new products.

Q. Was it the PMC-20 one of the new products you developed?

A. Yes.

Q. When did you conceive of the design for the PMC-20?

A. As best I can answer this question, I conceived of it in about the middle of October, 1995.

Q. What was the problem that led you to think of this extensible level?

A. I don't know that I could isolate it, sir.

Q. Can you give me some illustration of the problem?

A. Yes. There was a need, as I perceived it, for an extensible level that would not come apart, if you will, when extended too far. I wanted an extensible level with a lock.

Q. What made you think there was a need for this?

A. Even when I was working at Boeing we had a need to level many things that were very large. As you can imagine, aircraft are huge. In the construction business there are frequently long rungs of lumber that need to be leveled. It's more accurate to use a longer level, but that's impractical to carry around. Therefore I thought if we had an extensible level it would be more practical, but I did not want one that if you took it off the long horizontal rung of lumber and had it in a vertical orientation it would come apart. The part that came apart could fall down and hit someone. It just did not seem to me to be the best design. Thus, I thought of a locking extensible level.

Q. When did you have these thoughts?

A. I can't give you an exact date.

Q. Can you approximate for me?

A. As I told you, as best I can recall I conceived of this in about the middle of October 1995.

Q. When did you have the design completed?

A. Well, I can't be 100% sure, but I know it was completed by November 14, 1995.

Q. How can you be so sure about that date?

A. Because I saw a memo I wrote after the design was completed.

Q. I'm going to show you what I've marked as Plaintiff's Exhibit 7. Do you recognize this?

(Plaintiff's Exhibit Number 7
marked for identification)

A. Yes I do.

Q. What is it?

A. This is the finished design drawing for the PMC-20.

Q. Who drew it?

A. I did.
Q. When?
A. I can't tell you exactly, but I know it was completed November 14, 1995.
Q. How can you tell?
A. As I said earlier, I saw a memo from that date.
Q. I note that this drawing has a date box in the lower right-hand corner. Do you see that?
A. Yes.
Q. There's no date in there, correct?
A. Yes, that's correct.
Q. Can you tell me why there isn't a date in that box?
A. No.
Q. Was it your practice to date drawings that you had done?
A. At that time, I don't know.
Q. Is it your practice now?
A. Yes.
Q. Do you have an explanation as to why this drawing isn't dated?
A. No.
Q. Do you have any understanding at all as to why this drawing isn't dated?

A. Well, I was relatively new at the time, and I may not have been crossing all my t's and dotting my i's. Although the design was finished I wasn't sure we were going to manufacture exactly this design and I may have been waiting until I got some feedback to date the drawing. However, I just don't know.
Q. What did you do with respect to your design after you had completed it?
A. I'm not sure I know what you mean.
Q. Did you bring your design to the attention of your superiors?
A. Yes.
Q. What, if anything, did you tell them about it?
A. I told them that my design was fairly well finished.
Q. Did you tell them anything else? Strike that. Who did you tell.
A. Mr. Stu N. Nellis and Pete T. Lamp.
Q. Who is Mr. Nellis?
A. He was my boss.
Q. Who is Mr. Lamp?
A. He was another employee of Pacific Machine Corporation.
Q. Why did you tell Mr. Nellis?
A. Because he was my boss.

Q. Why did you tell Mr. Lamp?
A. Because Mr. Lamp was a patent agent.
Q. What does being a patent agent have to do with anything?
A. I was suggesting that we look into getting a patent.
Q. I'm going to show you what's been marked as Defendant's Exhibit 6. Did you write this? It is a memo dated November 14, 1995 from A.C. Edgar to S.N. Nellis and P.T. Lamp.
(Defendant's Exhibit NO. 6
Marked for identification.)
A. I don't recall.
Q. Is that your signature on the bottom?
A. It certainly appears to be the way I sign memos.
Q. Is the document in the form of the memos used in November 14, 1995?
A. Yes.
Q. Earlier you mentioned you had seen a memo that made you certain about the date of November 14, 1995. Is this the memo?
A. Yes.
Q. Was Mr. Nellis your boss at the time?
A. Yes.
Q. Was Mr. Lamp employed by the company at the time?

A. Yes.
Q. Do you have any reason whatsoever to doubt that you wrote this memo on or about November 14, 1995?
A. No.
Q. So when you just said you didn't know whether you wrote this what did you mean?
A. I don't remember writing this. I have no doubt that I did, I just don't have a specific recollection of writing it.
Q. So you don't deny writing it?
A. No, I don't deny it at all.
Q. And you think you did write it?
A. Yes, I think I probably did write it.
Q. Mr. Edgar, we can do this the easy way or the hard way, and I guess you want me to do it the hard way.
MR. JETSAM: Objection. Counsel there is no need to attempt to intimidate the witness. He answered your question exactly correctly as you phrased it. We will stipulate that Mr. Edgar wrote Defendant's Exhibit 6.
Q. Simple questions deserve simple answers. Convoluted answers to simple questions are what I mean by "the hard way." Let's go on.
Mr. Edgar, the second page of Defendant's Exhibit 6 is a drawing. Do you see that?

A. Yes.

Q. Did this drawing accompany the memo?

A. Yes.

Q. The memo, Defendant's Exhibit 6, refers in the re to "Patent Problem with PMC-20" Do you see that?

A. Yes.

Q. What does "Patent Problem" mean?

A. I don't know.

Q. What did you mean by it when you wrote it?

MR. JETSAM: Objection; asked and answered. Answer the question.

A. I don't know.

Q. Were you aware of any patent problems with the PMC-20 at the time?

A. No, at least not that I can recall.

Q. Do you have any explanation as to why it says "Patent Problem"?

A. Well, perhaps I always consider patents to be a problem. Patent lawyers seem to be a problem. I didn't know whether there was any company policy, so that might have been the problem. I just don't know.

Q. Did you receive a response to your memo, Defendant's Exhibit 6?

A. Yes.
Q. What was the response?
A. The response was that due to the weak economic position of the company we would not file for a patent application.
Q. Did PMC have a policy regarding patents at the time?
A. Regarding patents, generally? I'm not sure I understand.
Q. Did PMC have a policy regarding filing for patents on inventions made by its employees at the time you wrote the memo, Defendant's Exhibit 6?
A. I seem to recall that we did.
Q. What was the policy?
A. I seemed to recall that the policy was not to file for patents.
Q. I'm showing you what has been marked as Defendant's Exhibit 7. Do you recognize this?
(Defendant's Exhibit NO. 7 Marked for identification.)
A. Yes.
Q. What is it?
A. A memo.
Q. From whom?

A. My boss, Mr. Nellis.
Q. To whom?
A. To me and to Mr. Lamp.
Q. Did you receive this on or about the date indicated on the document, November 15, 1995.
A. I don't recall specifically, but I expect I did. I have no reason to doubt it. You see, I'm not trying to be difficult.
Q. Was this memo kept by PMC in the ordinary course of its business?
A. I don't know what you mean, but it was in a file at PMC and during discovery in this case I located the file and gave it to our lawyers.
Q. Thank you. Is that Mr. Nellis' signature on the bottom?
A. Yes.
Q. Did you have any reason to doubt Mr. Nellis' explanation?
A. It was not my position to doubt or not doubt. I accepted his explanation.
Q. Did you have any reason to disagree with Mr. Nellis?
A. Again, I don't know that it was my job to agree or disagree. He was my boss, sir, and I did what he told me to.

Page 18

Kessling Deposition Services
206-555-1234

Q. Did he tell you anything else at that time with respect to the PMC-20?
A. Yes.
Q. What?
A. He told me to work with the engineering folks to begin to have it manufactured.
Q. Did he tell you to do anything else with respect to a possible patent on the PMC-20?
A. No.
Q. Did you work with the engineering folks to bring production of the PMC-20 into existence?
A. Yes.
Q. What did you do?
A. We did the normal engineering work feeding up to the production of a product.
Q. When did you roll out the PMC-20?
A. By about June 1996 we were in our initial production rungs.
Q. I'm showing you what I have marked as Defendant's Exhibit 8. Do you recognize this?

(Defendant's Exhibit NO. 8 marked for identification.)

A. Yes.

Q. What is it?
A. It's a memo from Mr. Nellis to me.?
Q. Did you receive this on or about May 24, 1996? The date indicated?
A. Yes.
Q. Is this a document kept by the company in the ordinary course of business?
A. Again, it was in our files. I'm not sure what you mean by "ordinary course of business" but it was a regular document kept in our files concerning the PMC-20.
Q. I note that Mr. Nellis advises you that you were anticipating orders of about 3,000 units by the end of June.
A. I see that.
Q. Was that true?
A. Yes, we had an initial rung of about 1,000 units and gave away 300 as promotional items.
Q. Who did you give them to?
A. Crew chiefs, construction personnel, distributors, stores that dealt with tools, particularly for the professional trades, and so forth.
Q. What was the reaction?
A. The reaction was great. That's why we thought we'd be selling about 3,000 units a month so early in the production

rung. Even at that rate we couldn't keep up with the demand because we could hardly make them. We were anticipating expanding our operations.

Q. Would you say that the PMC-20 was a commercial success?

A. It was successful for us, that's for sure.

Q. Was it successful in the marketplace?

A. All I know is we were selling more and more. As this exhibit, Defendant's Exhibit 8 points out we were anticipating orders that even outstripped our planning and production estimates.

Q. You know what a commercial success is, don't you Mr. Edgar?

A. I think I do.

Q. What is it, as you understand it?

A. It's when a product that you begin to offer for sale meets or exceeds your expectations.

Q. Did the PMC-20 meet or exceed your expectations?

A. Yes.

Q. I'd like to ask you some questions about Mr. Cooley, Mr. Parish, and their patent. At the time you designed your PMC-20 had you ever heard of Mr. Cooley?

A. No sir.

Q. Had you ever heard of Mr. Parrish?
A. No sir.
Q. Had you ever heard of their design for an extendable level?
A. No sir.
Q. By the time you started selling your PMC-20 did you know that a patent application had been filed by Mr. Cooley and Mr. Parrish for their design?
A. No sir.
Q. At the time you designed your level had you ever seen an extensible level?
A. No sir.
Q. Had you ever heard of one?
A. Well, I understood from discussions with some other folks that they existed, but that's about all.
Q. Had you ever heard of the Bullivant Company?
A. I don't recall that I did.
Q. At the time you did your work had you ever seen the Bullivant `524 patent, which has been marked as Defendant's Exhibit 1?
A. No sir.
Q. All right, I'd like to change topics for a minute. There came a time when the company was accused of patent

SECTION G

infringement. Do you recall that?

A. Yes sir.

Q. When was that?

A. I can't give you an exact date, but it was in the Fall of 1999.

Q. I want to show you what is marked as Defendant's Exhibit 5. Do you recognize this?

(Defendant's Exhibit NO. 5 marked for identification.)

A. Yes I do.

Q. What is it?

A. It's a memo.

Q. For the record it is a memo on Pacific Machine Corporation memo paper dated October 18, 1999, purporting to be from Mr. M.C. Pringle to Mr. S.N. Nellis, Mr. A.C. Edgar, Mr. Pete T. Lamp regarding "Patent Problem with PMC-20" is that correct?

A. Yes.

Q. Did you receive this on or about October 18, 1999?

A. I assume I did.

Q. I note that the re line refers to a "Patent Problem." That's the same re line you used in your memo in 1995, Defendant's Exhibit 6. Isn't it?

A. Yes.

Q. Does that refresh your recollection that you were aware of the design and possible patenting by Mr. Cooley and Mr. Parrish as early 1995?

A. No, I don't believe I did.

MR. JETSAM: Objection. Counsel, as you are aware, the application for the `056 patent was not even filed by the time he wrote that memo on November 14, 1995. Your question is unfair.

MR. ADAMS: Well, he answered it. I'll go on.

Q. This memo of October 18, 1999, Defendant's Exhibit 5, says that you have received a letter from Bullivant Tool accusing you of patent infringement. Do you see that?

A. Yes.

Q. It goes on to say that your attorneys ask that you gather all the information you have on the design and development of the PMC-20. Do you see that?

A. Yes.

Q. Did you do so?

A. Yes, as I said earlier, I gathered these materials together and gave them to our lawyers.

Q. It also refers to a meeting to take place the following Thursday, do you see that?

A. Yes. It was later that week.
Q. Did you have such a meeting?
A. Yes we did.
Q. What did you discuss?
MR. JETSAM: Objection. Privileged. You need not answer that.
Q. Let me ask it differently. Or rather let me ask you a different question. Was your counsel present at that meeting?
A. Yes.
Q. Do you recall what was discussed?
A. Yes.
Q. Without giving the specifics can you give me the general subject matter of the discussion?
MR. JETSAM: Objection. Privileged. I'll allow him to answer generally if you will agree that it does not constitute a waiver of the attorney/client privilege.
MR. ADAMS: Yes, I'll agree. I just want in overall terms the general subject matter.
MR. JETSAM: Okay, you can answer generally.
A. Generally, we discussed the accusation of patent infringement brought by Bullivant. We discussed what we should do, and there was some back and forth, give and take, where we all expressed our opinions concerning the appropriate action to

be followed. Mind you, I was just an engineering, and this seemed to me to be a decision for management and the lawyers. So I didn't think I really had much of a role in the decision as to what was to be done, I was just there to give input. But generally, the subject was the claim of infringement.

MR. JETSAM: Thank you Mr. Edgar. That's enough. I think you've answered his question and any further information about the subject would improperly invade the attorney/client privilege.

MR. ADAMS: Okay, no further questions.

CROSS EXAMINATION BY MR. JETSAM

Q. Mr. Edgar, you indicated at one time that you thought a patent should be applied for. Do you still hold that view?

A. Well, I don't know that I ever really held the view. In retrospect I think adding a locking mechanism to an extensible level would have been a pretty obvious thing.

Q. Obvious to whom?

A. Well, to anyone, sir. It readily occurred to me, and I think it would have been obvious to just about anybody trying to design a level.

MR. ADAMS: Objection. This man isn't tendered as an expert witness, and here he is giving opinion testimony.

MR. JETSOM: I'm just following up on the questions you

Page 26

Kessling Deposition Services
206-555-1234

asked about the suggestion that they seek a patent.

MR. ADAMS: I simply asked him about memos he wrote, I didn't go into any opinion testimony.

MR. JETSOM: I'll move on.

Q. Why did you suggest filing a patent application on the level, as reflected in the exhibits you were asked about on direct examination, Defendant's Exhibit 6?

A. When I worked at Boeing the patent attorneys patented everything under the sun, or at least they seemed to. Any time we had any idea we were urged to contact the Patent Department, and they filed more patent applications than we sold airplanes.

Q. Can you give me any examples?

A. Well, one of the things I worked on was a little tool to help position the lights in the floor to guide passengers to an exit. The tool was just like the thing you use to put a bicycle inner tube on the rim of a bicycle wheel before you put the tire over it. It was a very simple tool. They even tried to patent that.

Q. Did they get a patent?

A. I don't think so. At least they didn't tell me about it.

Q. What about the level you designed, which became the PMC-20?

A. There are probably as many possible ways to make a brake or stop to lock the device as there are engineers. Their goal was simply to prevent movement of the sliding member of the level. All I did was pick what I thought was best suited to my particular design, to the sliding member of my PMC-20.

Q. Was the selection you made an obvious one?

MR. ADAMS: Objection, calls for legal conclusion.

MR. JETSAM: You can answer.

A. It seemed obvious to me.

Q. You indicated that you received Mr. Nellis' explanation, the memo of Defendant's Exhibit 7, dated November 15, 1995. That's the one that says that due to economic conditions there was a policy of not filing patents. Do you recall that?

A. Yes.

Q. You also said that you did not consider it your job to disagree with your boss, do you recall that?

A. Yes.

Q. Did you, in fact, agree with his decision?

A. I suppose I did. I certainly went along with it.

MR. JETSAM: No further questions.

MR. ADAMS: I have some questions on redirect.

Q. Mr. Edgar turning to Defendant's Exhibit 7, did you

have a discussion with Mr. Nellis at the time of his memo?

A. Yes.

Q. What was Mr. Nellis' position?

A. He was Director of Sales of Pacific Machine Corporation.

Q. During that discussion did you urge that the policy of not filing for patents be reviewed?

A. Yes I did.

Q. What were the bases for your suggestions or urging that the policy be reviewed?

A. Since Pete Lamp was a patent agent I though it could be done relatively cheaply or even at no cost to the company.

Q. What was Mr. Lamp's job?

A. He was Production Manager for PMC.

Q. How did you know he was a registered patent agent?

A. Pete and I worked together routinely. He just mentioned he was a patent agent and I thought that meant he could prepare patent applications. It didn't seem that hard to do from my perspective, and I thought he could do it in his spare time.

Q. Did you express this view to Mr. Nellis?

A. I'm sure I did.

Q. What was his response?

A. Well, our conversation was primarily one of policy, and his answer was we simply didn't have very much extra money.
Q. During that discussion did you focus at all on the design of your new level?
A. In part we discussed the design of the level, sure.
Q. Did Mr. Nellis offer a view on the patentability of the design?
A. I don't recall that he did.
Q. Did you?
A. Well, I don't know how to answer that.
Q. Why do you say that?
A. Obviously I was asking that we file for a patent on the design but I can't say I thought it was patentable. You can file for a patent and sometimes it gets rejected. But I thought if Mr. Lamp could do so cheaply we'd have very little to lose. So when you say did I express a view about whether or not the design was patentable I'd have to say no. At least I don't recall. But did I express a view about whether we should file for a patent? Sure, if it was cheap and easy, why not do it? That was my thought, at least. That's how we operated at Boeing. But like I said, I was new at PMC, I wasn't about to rock the boat.
MR. ADAMS: No further questions, that's the end of the

deposition, thank you.

(Deposition adjourned at 12:12 p.m.)

(Signature waived.)

CERTIFICATE OF COURT REPORTER

UNITED STATES OF AMERICA)

STATE OF WASHINGTON)

I, Kathy Geyne Kessling, the reporter before whom the foregoing deposition was taken, do hereby certify that the witness whose testimony appears in the foregoing deposition was sworn by me; that the testimony of said witness was taken by me in machine shorthand and thereafter transcribed by computer-aided transcription; that said deposition is a true record of the testimony given by said witness; that I am neither counsel for, related to, nor employed by any of the parties to the action in which this deposition was taken; and, further, that I am not a relative or employee of any attorney or counsel employed by the parties hereto, or financial or otherwise interested in the outcome of this action.

KATHY GEYNE KESSLING

Notary Public in and for the

State of Washington

My Commission Expires August 5, 2006

Witness Name: Alan C. Edgar
Volume:
Re: Bullivant Tools v. Pacific Machine Corporation

Deposition Date: June 8, 2005
Court Reporter: Kathy Geyne Kessling
Case No. 04-9876

Page	Line	Correction

I hereby certify that I have read the foregoing deposition, and that this deposition, together with any corrections, is a true and accurate record of my testimony given at this deposition.

____
Witness's Signature

Subscribed and sworn to before me this _______day

of _________________, 20______.

____
Notary Public:
My Commission Expires:

SECTION G-4

IN THE UNITED STATES DISTRICT COURT FOR WASHINGTON

WESTERN DISTRICT

Bullivant Tool, Inc.,)

Plaintiff,) Case No. 04 9876

v.)

Pacific Machine Corporation)

Defendant.)

VIDEOTAPED DEPOSITION OF SUSAN S. PARRISH

Thursday, August 18, 2005

Reported by: Kathy G. Kessling, RPR

The videotaped deposition of Susan S. Parrish, a witness herein, was convened on Thursday, August 18, 2005, commencing at 9:08 a.m., at the offices of Flotsam & Jetsam, 98765 Ocean Avenue, Seattle, Washington, 98120, before Kathy Geyne Kessling, Registered Professional Reporter.

APPEARANCES

For Plaintiff:
MR. AMOS A. ADAMS, Esquire
1000 Japan Trade Building
Seattle, Washington 98120
Telephone: 206-354-2400

For Defendant:
CHARLES F. JETSAM, Esquire
Flotsam & Jetsam
98765 Ocean Avenue
Seattle, Washington 98120
Telephone: 206-354-2800

Also present: T.J. Sullivan, Videographer

Page 3

Kessling Deposition Services
206-555-1234

CONTENTS

EXHIBITS

(Exhibits retained by counsel.)

PROCEEDINGS

THE VIDEOGRAPHER: On the record with Tape Number 1 of the videotape deposition of Susan A. Parrish, taken by the Defendant in the matter of Bullivant Tool, Inc., versus Pacific Machine Corporation in the United States District Court for Washington, Eastern District, Case Number 04 9876.

This Deposition is being held at the law offices of Flotsam & Jetsam, 98765 Ocean Avenue, Seattle, Washington, 98120, on August 16, 2004, at approximately 9:08 a.m.

My name is T.J. Sullivan, representing Kessling Deposition Services. I'm a certified legal video specialist.

The court reporter is Kathy Geyne Kessling representing Kessling Deposition Services. I'm a certified court reporter.

Will counsel please introduce themselves and indicate which parties they represent.

MR. JETSAM: I am Charles F. Jetsam, counsel for Pacific Machine Corporation.

MR. ADAMS: And I am Mr. Adams, and I represent Bullivant Tool, Inc.

SUSAN A. PARRISH,

called for examination, having been first duly sworn, was examined and testified as follows;

EXAMINATION BY COUNSEL FOR PACIFIC MACHINE CORPORATION BY Mr. Jetsam.

Q. Good morning Mrs. Parrish. My name is Charles Jetsam and I'll be taking this deposition. Have you ever been deposed before?

A. No.

Q. There's no need to be nervous. I'll simply be asking you some questions that you'll have to answer. You understand you are under oath. Right?

A. Yes.

Q. After I ask the question you will simply have to provide me an answer unless your lawyer makes an objection and tells you not to answer the question.

A. Okay.

Q. If I ask you any questions that are confusing to you, please let me know. I want this to be as clear as possible for both of us.

A. Yes, that's fair.

Q. If you answer a question I ask you we will assume that you understood it so if you don't understand the question, please say so.

A. Okay.

Q. If you need a break of need to consult with your

lawyer at any time, just let me know. The only thing I ask is that you not ask for a break or consult with your lawyer while a question is pending. The only exception is if you think my question may be asking you to tell me about a conversation you've had with your lawyers, although I don't think I'll ask any such questions. Do you understand that?

A. Yes.

Q. One other thing. You'll notice we have a court reporter here as well as a videographer. Before you start to answer a question, please be sure I've finished it. Also, if your attorney starts to speak and make an objection please give him an opportunity to finish because it is very difficult for the court reporter if two people are speaking at once.

A. Okay.

Q. Would you like anything to drink?

A. No I'm fine.

Q. We have some water and pop over there. So if you want anything just let us know and if you would like some juice we can probably can get that.

A. Fine, thank you. Maybe a little later.

Q. Mrs. Parrish, when were you born?

A. Right out of the box you have to ask me a question I don't want to answer. (Laughter.) I was born July 6, 1960.

Page 7

Kessling Deposition Services
206-555-1234

Q. Can you tell me a little bit about your education.
A. I graduated from St. Sebastian High School in Columbus, Ohio in June 1977. I then went to the Ohio State Hospital for the Mentally Ill in Columbus, Ohio. I was in a two-year nurse's training program there, and got my certificate.
Q. When did you leave the Ohio State Hospital?
A. I worked there until May 1980. I got my certificate in June of `79, and continued to work at the hospital until the next May.
Q. Why did you leave?
A. I left to marry George. After we were married I did not work.
Q. By George you mean . . .
A. My late husband, George Parrish.
Q. When were you married?
A. June 14, 1980.
Q. When did you first meet George, Mr. Parrish?
A. I met him in late winter of 1978, it had to be around March. He was home from leave from the Army and we met at a dance.
Q. When were you married?
A. We were married on June 14, 1980.
Q. Oh I'm sorry. You just said that. Do you have any

children?

A. We have three children.

Q. Since you left working, what have you done?

A. I have been a stay-at-home mom. I stayed home raising our children until after George's death, when I had to return to work.

Q. When did you return to work?

A. I returned to work in the Spring of 1999.

Q. Where did you go to work?

A. I returned to work as a nurse full time at the Ohio State Hospital.

Q. Are you still employed there now?

A. Yes, that is where I work.

Q. I'd like to ask you a few questions about your husband's estate, your late husband's estate. Who was the executor of the estate?

A. I was named the executor of the estate.

Q. What did you understand your duties to be?

A. Well, I worked with a lawyer to wind up his estate in an orderly fashion. There really wasn't much to do as George was always pretty organized, but I had to sign some papers, review a bunch a papers, and give the lawyer all the things that related to the business and so forth.

Q. When you say you had to review the papers, what did you mean?

A. George kept a bunch of stuff at home, and some of it related to the business of course. So I went through his papers and if it looked interesting or important I either gave it to the lawyer or I gave it to Charley Cooley, who essentially took over the business as President. I stayed on as one of the co-owners.

Q. I'd like to show you what's been marked as Defendant's Exhibit 4. Do you recognize this?

A. Yes, I do, although . . .

MR. JETSAM: I'll get to how you found it. But I just want to know whether you recognize what it is.

A. Yes I do.

Q. Is this one of the letters you found in your husband's estate?

A. Well, I don't know how to answer that.

Q. Why not?

A. It's one of the letters I found, but I did not find it, or at least I don't remember finding it, in connection with cleaning up George's estate. I might have found it then, but I really didn't pay very much attention to it if I did because it was in a file that seemed to deal only in the history of the

Parrish Construction Company. It had a bunch of letters and notes and newspaper clippings about big jobs they did and things like that. It didn't seem to be a business item so I didn't give it to the lawyer, at least I don't think I did. I don't think I paid any attention to it at all, to tell you the truth. I just put it back.

Q. When you say put it back, what do you mean?

A. I just put it back in the file and stuck it back in the box in the basement. I didn't throw it out or anything like that. In fact I didn't throw out any of the files of George. I don't know why I didn't, I just didn't. I kept thinking I should do so and promised myself I would do so if I ever moved, but I never moved.

Q. Are you still living in the same house you lived in when George was alive.

A. Yes. I didn't move because I didn't want to change the children's schools. I don't know, I just didn't feel like moving.

Q. When do you recall doing anything with this exhibit, Defendant's Exhibit 4?

A. Well after I heard about the lawsuit, this lawsuit about the patent and the patent on the level, I seemed to recall this letter. So I . . .

Q. When you say "this letter" you're referring to Defendant's Exhibit 4?

A. Yes. I seem to recall Defendant's Exhibit 4, the letter from George's grandfather. So I went down into the basement and scouted around among his things and found it.

Q. What did you do with it?

A. I sent it to Charley.

Q. By Charley you mean . . .

A. Charley Cooley. He was President of the company, the construction company, and one of the inventors. Since I thought it might relate to the patent lawsuit I thought it would be important in some way. So I sent it on to him.

Q. I'm going to show you what is marked as Defendant's Exhibit 3, an e-mail dated December 10, 2004. Did you write this e-mail?

A. Yes.

Q. Did you write this on December 10, 2004?

A. Yes. This is the e-mail I sent to Charley when I found the other letter, Defendant's Exhibit 4.

Q. I note that your e-mail to Mr. Cooley says that George's grandfather was, and I'll quote "a little eccentric but a nice old gentleman." Did you write that?

A. Yes I did.

Q. What did you mean by that?

A. Well, George's grandfather was a really nice gentleman. But he had a very vivid imagination and sometimes you weren't entirely sure that what he was saying was entirely correct.

Q. Was he a liar?

A. No, I don't mean that. You know, I'm a nurse in this area and sometimes patients, due to their advanced age and the presence of artiosclerosis, they get a little imaginative. This tends to become more pronounced over time, and I certainly think that was true with George's grandfather. During the last five to eight years of his life he tended to, well, exaggerate some things and imagine other things as true. I don't mean that in any negative way. He wasn't a liar or anything and he probably didn't even know he was doing it. It's just that, well, he had a vivid imagination.

Q. When did he die?

A. He died in 1997.

Q. I have no further questions at this time.

CROSS-EXAMIANTION BY Mr. ADAMS

Q. Mrs. Parrish, I'd like to ask you a few questions about your late husband's grandfather. You said he had a vivid imagination. Can you expand on that a bit? Given your professional background.

A. Well during the years prior to his death he occasionally made up stories. These were harmless stories, they really didn't amount to anything, but they were made up.

Q. Can you give us an example?

A. One time he came in and just told a story about taking the children to a carnival in town that day. Well, there was no carnival in town. It was pretty clear to me he was remembering a carnival he had attended as a child because the attractions were not the kind of thing that kids today would go to. This was totally harmless, but it just wasn't true. He had been with them at soccer practice, and I took him, but there was no carnival. This is the type of thing he would do.

Q. Was Mr. Parrish's grandfather always in this state?

A. Oh no. Many times he had a vivid and accurate recall of events. Sometimes he was quite lucid. Probably most of the time. However there were times he was completely out of touch with reality. This is just the way it is with people having his condition.

Q. When you say he was sometimes probably more lucid - strike that. When you say he was probably more often vivid and accurate, what do you base that on?

A. Actually, I think it would be correct to say that more

often than not he made up stories, harmless ones, but he did it quite frequently towards the end of his life. It really was both sad and amusing, because he was such a nice gentleman. However, he probably made up stories more often than not during the last few years of his life.

Q. Turning to Defendant's Exhibit 4, are you aware of any of the facts in that letter?

A. Well, he references George being in the Army, and I certainly know that. But as a practical matter, no I don't know whether that letter is true or not. I just wasn't around, you see.

Q. Do you know anyone who was?

A. Who was what?

Q. Who was around, who could tell us whether the story in that letter about the adjustable level is true?

A. No, I don't know anyone who could speak to that.

Q. Were there any other letters in the file or in your late husband's materials that related to adjustable levels?

A. No. After this became an issue, you know, I went down and searched through all the other documents to see if there were any other letters or drawings or other materials that might shed some light on this. I could not find anything else. As I said this was just in a file of stuff about the construction company, not about the levels per se.

Q. Can you tell me a little bit about the relationship between your husband and Mr. Cooley, Charley Cooley?

A. Oh they were great friends.

Q. For how long?

A. For as long as I've known them. They were friends when I met George. As I understood it they had gone to high school together and joined the Army together.

Q. When you knew them what was their relationship?

A. They were great friends. They would go out bowling for the company bowling team. They often went out for a beer together. We barbequed together as families. It was a normal friendly relationship between two guys who worked together and who liked working together. Our families were friends, and still are.

Q. Mrs. Parrish, do you know where one could find levels, adjustable levels, actually constructed by your husband?

A. No, I really don't where they are. This really was George and Charley fooling around in the workshop.

Q. When you say "in the workshop," what do you mean?

A. We have a workshop in the basement of our home. I should say we had one, not have one. I gave the tools to Charley. When they were working on their level they would go

down there and do whatever they did.
Q. Do you know how the levels worked?
A. The ones they made?
Q. Yes.
A. Not really.
Q. What can you tell me about them?
A. I know he was always taking about it, but I never paid much attention to the business and it seemed to me to be the kind of thing that interested them more than me.
Q. Could you identify one of the levels he made if you saw it?
A. Probably not. They all look alike to me.
Q. When you say "they all look alike" what are you referring to?
A. Oh, you know, their tools. Levels and adjustable levels and regular levels and chisels and planes and all this stuff that they're always dragging around. I never really paid any attention to it. It's all just dirty stuff to me.
Q. Thank you Mrs. Parrish, I have no further questions.
THE VIDOGRAPHER: This ends Tape Number 1 and concludes the testimony of Susan A. Parrish in the matter of Bullivant Tool versus Pacific Machine Corporation.
The date is August 18, 2005, the time is 10:12:02. Off the

Page 17

Kessling Deposition Services
206-555-1234

record.

(Deposition adjourned at 10:12 a.m.)

(Signature waived.)

CERTIFICATE OF COURT REPORTER

UNITED STATES OF AMERICA)

STATE OF WASHINGTON)

I, Kathy Geyne Kessling, the reporter before whom the foregoing deposition was taken, do hereby certify that the witness whose testimony appears in the foregoing deposition was sworn by me; that the testimony of said witness was taken by me in machine shorthand and thereafter transcribed by computer-aided transcription; that said deposition is a true record of the testimony given by said witness; that I am neither counsel for, related to, nor employed by any of the parties to the action in which this deposition was taken; and, further, that I am not a relative or employee of any attorney or counsel employed by the parties hereto, or financial or otherwise interested in the outcome of this action.

KATHY GEYNE KESSLING

Notary Public in and for the

State of Washington

My Commission Expires August 5, 2006

Page 19

Kessling Deposition Services
206-555-1234

Witness Name: Susan A. Parrish
Volume:
Re: Bullivant Tools v.
Pacific Machine Corporation

Deposition Date: August 18, 2005
Court Reporter: Kathy Geyne Kessling
Case No. 04-9876

Page	Line	Correction

I hereby certify that I have read the foregoing deposition, and that this deposition, together with any corrections, is a true and accurate record of my testimony given at this deposition.

____
Witness's Signature

Subscribed and sworn to before me this _______day

of _________________, 20______.

____
Notary Public:
My Commission Expires:

Section H

Exhibits Premarked By Plaintiff

(No Stipulations)

SECTION NO. **Page**

SECTION H-1

United States Patent [19] | [11] **Patent Number: 5,624,056**

Parrish et al. | [45] **Date of Patent: Apr. 22, 1997**

[54] **ADJUSTABLE PLUMB AND LEVEL**

[75] Inventors: **George L. Parrish; Charley A. Cooley**, all of Columbus, Ohio

[73] Assignee:

[21] Appl. No.: 452,879

[22] Filed: March 20, 1996

References Cited

U.S. PATENT DOCUMENTS

5,351,524 1/1960 Bullivant

ABSTRACT

This invention is an apparatus that relates to plumbs and levels and is capable of being adjusted to a length desired. The apparatus has a movable extension capable of increasing the length of the plumb and level without destroying its shape. It also has a movable extension slidable on the support of the plumb and level glasses without interfering with the adjustment of the glasses.

The apparatus has a body member, that has the plumb and level glasses adjustably mounted and where one end of the body member is movable away from and toward the body member of the medium of arms slidable in channels formed in opposite faces of the body member. The body member is also capable of providing plumb and level glasses that are adjustably mounted and where one end of the body member is movable away from and toward the body member to the medium of arms slidable in channels formed in opposite faces of the body member.

1 Claim, 8 drawings

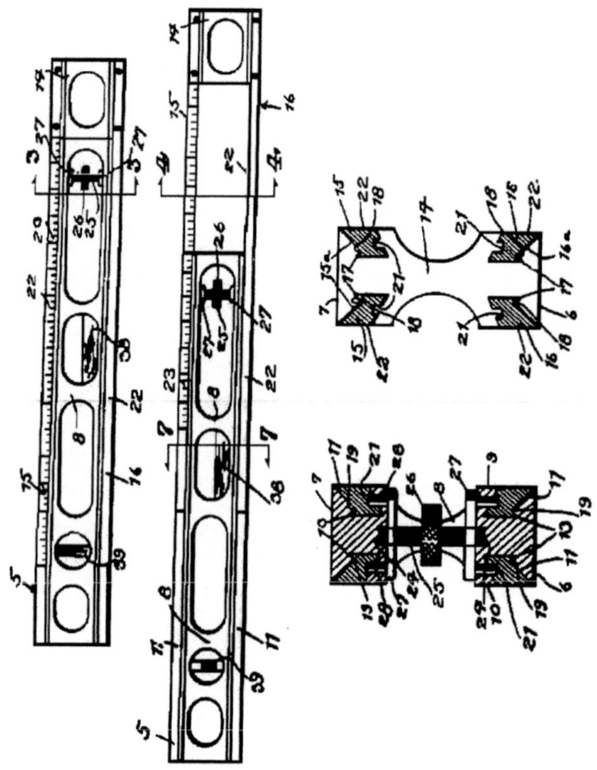

PLAINTIFF'S EXHIBIT

No. 1

U.S. Patent April 22, 1997 Sheet 1 of 2 **5,624,056**

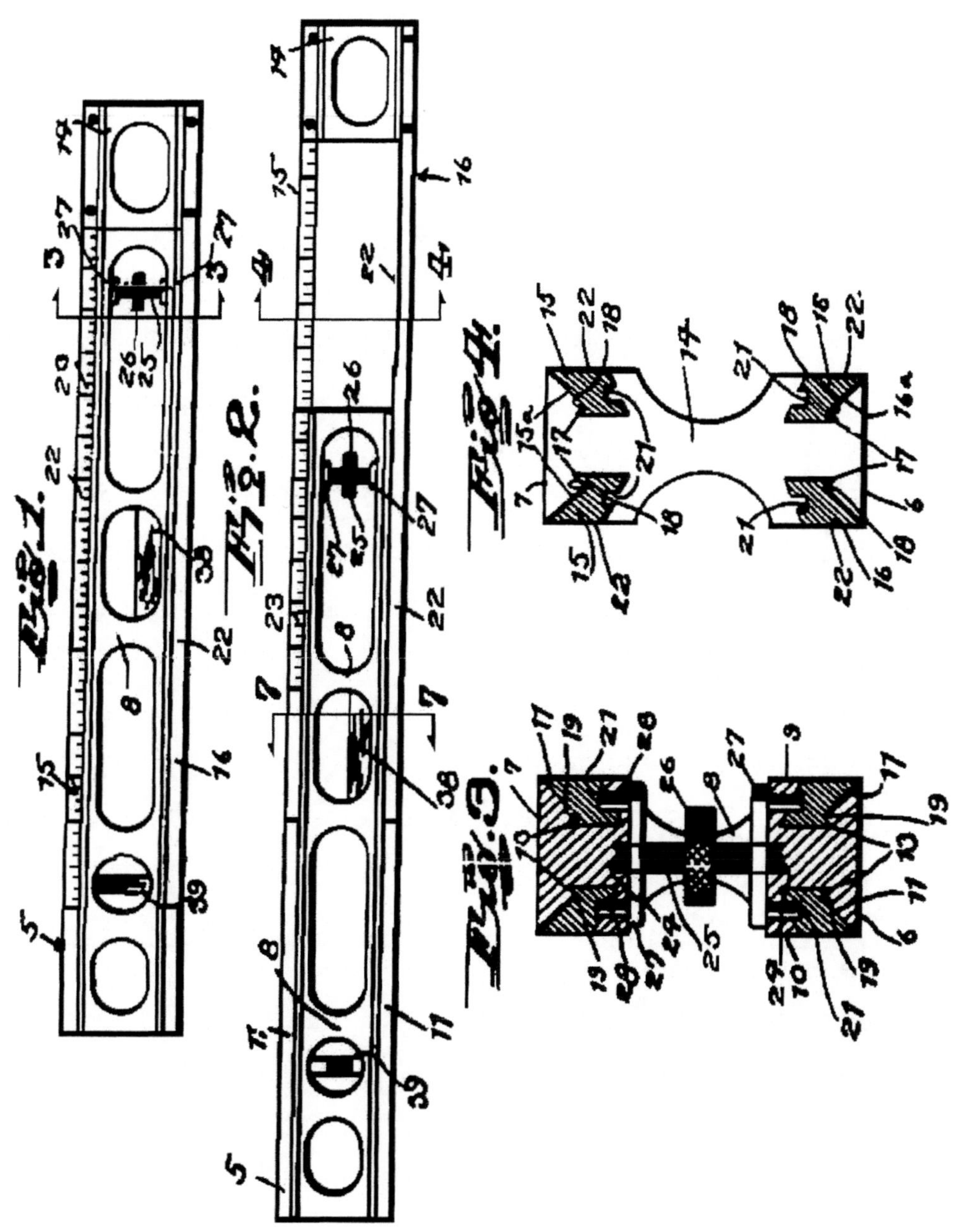

U.S. Patent April 22, 1997 Sheet 2 of 2 **5,624,056**

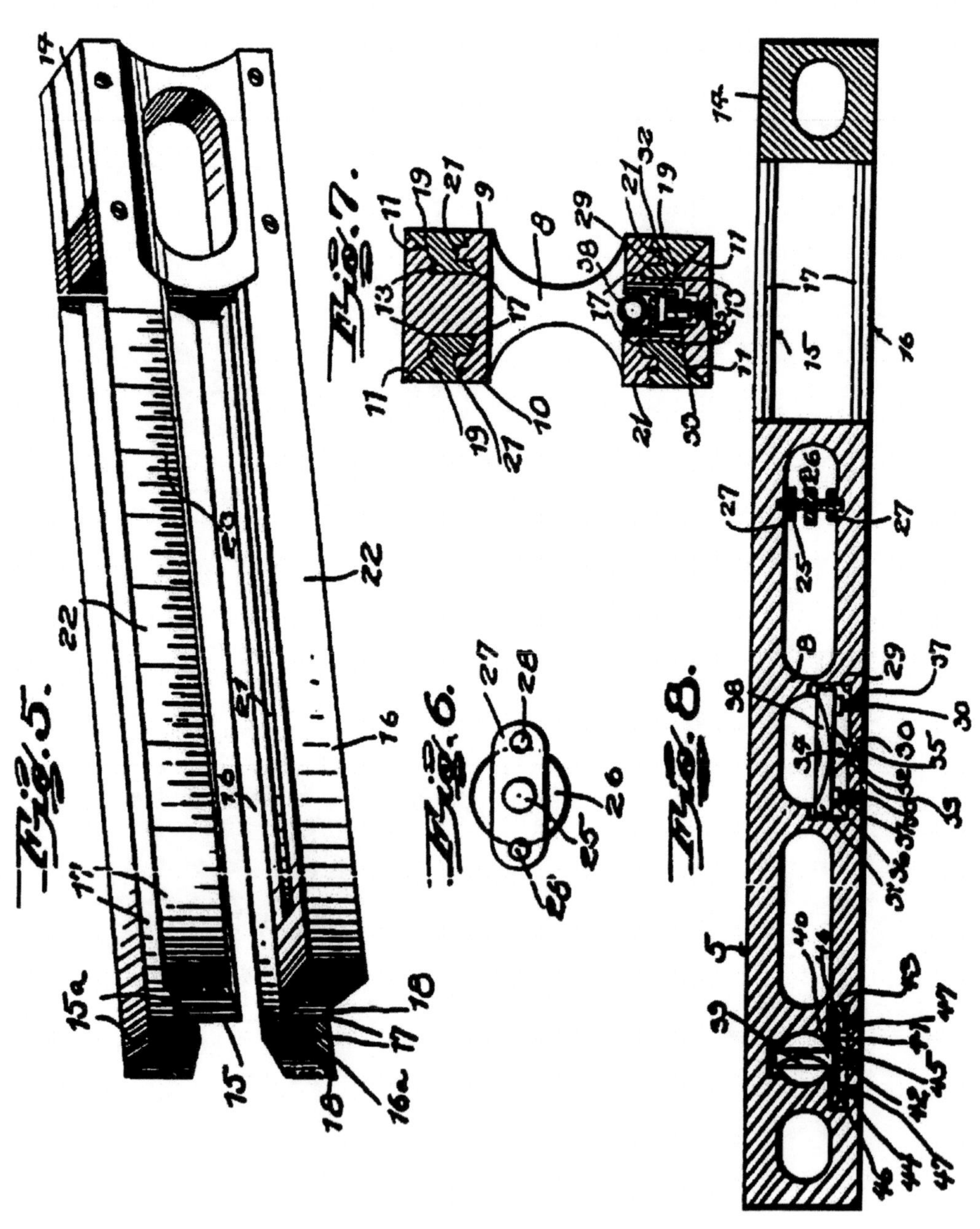

5,624,056

1

FIELD OF THE INVENTION

This invention relates to new and useful Improvements in Adjustable Plumbs and Levels.

SUMMARY OF THE INVENTION

This invention relates to plumbs and levels, and has for its object to provide a device of this character capable of being adjusted to the length desired.

Another object is to provide a device of this character including a movable extension capable of increasing the length of the plumb and level without destroying the shape thereof.

Another object is to provide a device of this character including a movable extension slidable on the support of the plumb and level glasses without interfering with the adjustment of the glasses.

A still further object of the invention is to provide a device of this character including a body member in which plumb and level glasses are adjustably mounted and wherein one end of the body member is movable away from and toward the body member of the medium of arms slidable in channels formed in opposite faces of the body member.

A still further object of the invention is to provide a device of this character including a body member in which plumb and level glasses are adjustably mounted and wherein one end of the body member is movable away from and toward the body member to the medium of arms slidable in channels formed in opposite faces of the body member.

A still further object of the invention is to provide a device of this character wherein the body member is provided with mans adapted to secure the extension in its adjusted position.

DESCRIPTION OF THE DRAWINGS

With these and other objects in view, the invention consists in the improved construction and arrangement of parts to be hereinafter more particularly described, fully claimed and illustrated in the accompanying drawings, in which:

Figure 1 is a side elevation of a plumb and level in its closed position,

Figure 2 is a side elevation of a plumb and level showing the extension in use,

Figure 3 is a section taken on the line 3—3 of Figure 1,

Figure 4 is a section taken on the line 4—4 of Figure 2,

Figure 5 is a perspective view of the extension,

Figure 6 is a plan view of the locking mechanism,

Figure 7 is a section taken on the line 7—7 of Figure 2, and

Figure 8 is a longitudinal sectional view of the structure shown in Figure 2.

DESCRIPTION OF THE PREFERRED EMBODIMENT

Referring to the drawings, 5 designates a body member formed from a single piece of material and including opposed work engaging faces 6i and 7, said faces being connected by mans of webs 8. The sides 9 and 10 of the body member adjacent the faces 5 and 6 are provided and channels 11, two channels being provided in each side. The channel extends upwardly and forwardly, and longitudinally of the body member 5. The outer wall 12 of the channel 11 is undercut to provide a channel 13, which serves to prevent lateral movement of an extension, the channel 13 being substantially V-shaped.

In order to increase the length of the body member 5,

2

there is provided a novel extension, which consists of a body member or block 14 adapted to coincide with the end face of the body member and adapted to form one end of the body member. The block 14 is provided with a plurality of arms 15 and 16, one arm extending from each longitudinal corner or edge of the block. Each of the arms 15 has its face 15^a inclined inwardly and downwardly while the lower face 16^a of the arms 16 are inclined upwardly, the inner portions of said faces terminating below the inner edge thereof to provide a flange 17 and a channel 18. The flange 17 is adapted to be disposed in the channel 18, while the channel 18 is adapted to receive the ridge 19 formed at the junction of the channel 18 and the outer wall of the channel 11. The lower faces of the arms 15 and upper faces of the arms 16 are provided with grooves 21, said grooves extending longitudinally of the arms and terminating adjacent one end thereof to provide a stop. It will be noted that the lower faces of the arms 15 and upper faces of the arms 16 extend in parallel relation to the opposite faces of said arms. By this novel arrangement, the arms 15 and 16 are permitted to slide in the channels 11 longitudinally of the body member 5, lateral movement of said arms being prevented through the cooperation of the channel 13 and the flange 17, it being of course obvious that sufficient play is allowed to prevent the binding of the arms within the channels 11. 1

It will be noted that the outer face 22 of each arm is disposed closely adjacent the work engaging faces 6 and 7, and in right angular relation to said faces. The grooves 21 terminate adjacent the ends of the arms to prevent disengagement of the arms. The channels 11 and the arms, in view of their interlocking engagement, will eliminate the necessity of depending upon the block 14 to maintain the arms 15 and 16 in a true position when the extension is in use, and it is desired to obtain the exact level of work on which the device is used. The outer face 22 of each of the arms 15 is provided with a scale 23 which permits the operator to set the extension at the desired distance without the use of an additional or separate rule, it being also useful for other measuring purposes.

Projecting from the inner face of each of the work-engaging faces 6 and 7 is a socket 24, said sockets being disposed in opposed registering relation and between certain of the webs of the body member. These sockets are intended to receive the ends of a shaft 25, a knurled thumb nut 26 being secured to the intermediate portion of the shaft. The portion of the shaft on one side of the nut 26 is provided with right hand threads, while the remaining portion on the opposite side of the nut is provided with left hand threads. A locking plate 27, including a central threaded opening, is mounted on each threaded and portion of the shaft, the plates including fingers 28 adapted to extend through the inner wall of the channel into the grooves 21 of the arms 15, one finger being provided for each arm. It is of course obvious that when the shaft is rotated by means of the nut 26, in view of the right and left hand threads, the plate 27 will be moved toward or away from each other so as to cause the fingers 28 to extend into the grooves 21 and engage the arms 15. When the plates are moved away from each other toward the arms, the fingers come into binding engagement with the arms and thereby lock the same in their adjusted positions, movement of said plates toward each other releasing the arms to permit adjustment of the extension.

The intermediate portion of the body member 5 is provided with a channel 29, said channel having a plurality of openings 30. Disposed within the channel is a casing 31 having a pair of opposed ears 32 depending from the intermediate portion of the bottom of the casing. A socket member 33 is disposed between the ears 32, said socket member being interiorly threaded and having trunnions 34 projecting from one end thereof, said trunnions being journaled in the ears 32 to permit pivotal movement of the casing 31. A screw 35 is passed through one of the openings 30 into the socket member 33. Depending from the bottom of the casing 31 adjacent

5,624,056

3

each end thereof is a threaded socket 36, each socket being adapted to receive a screw 37, which are passed through the remaining openings 30. By means of the screws 37 the casing 31 may be adjusted to various inclinations. Mounted within the casing 31 is a bubble or spirit level glass 38.

Disposed in spaced relation to the spirit level glass 38 is a plumb glass 39. This glass is adjustable similar to the glass 38 by means consisting of a casing 40 adapted to receive the glass 39, said casing being secured to the intermediate portion of a plate 41, the plate 41 having a pair of ears 42 depending from its lower intermediate portion. The plate 41 is disposed within the channel 43 formed in the body member 5. Said channel, similar to the channel 29, is provided with a plurality of openings 44. A socket member 45 similar to the socket member 33 is disposed beneath the plate for pivotally supporting the same. The ends of the plate are provided with sockets 46 adapted to receive screws 47 by means of which the plate 41 may be disposed in various inclined positions.

By this novel device, it is possible to increase the length of the body member without causing any portion of the extension to overlap the body member. In addition to this, by the novel formation of the channel 11 and the arms 15 and 16, the shape and accuracy of the body member is not disturbed even

4

when the block 14 is disposed at the limit of its movement away from the body member 5. Furthermore, the arms 15 and 16 are disposed flush with the sides 9 and 10, no portion of the movable arms intersecting the work-engaging face of the body member, so that the extension may be operated even when the device is supported by the work, as the arms 15 and 16i do no t at any time engage the work. By a slight rotation of the shaft 215, the locking plates 17 are simultaneously moved to lock all of the arms of the extension in the desired adjusted position, the adjustable feature of the plumb and level glasses permitting the same to be maintained in various inclinations. The invention possesses every feature necessary to render a device of this character efficient and convenient for the user.

What is claimed is:

1. An extensible, non-overlapping plumb and level of the character described comprising a body member having channels in the side faces thereof, an extension disposed for sliding movement on the body member, said extension having arms slidable in the channels of the body member, and locking means carried by the body member for frictional engagement with the arms to selectively prevent movement of the extension.

SECTION H-2

Parrish Construction Company
600 Westerville Road
Columbus, Ohio
216-555-3411

September 2, 1996

Bullivant Tool Company
135 S. LaSalle Street
Chicago, IL

Gentlemen:

For a number of years, this company has given to each crew chief, a Bullivant model B-100 Extension Level as a gift upon completion of three years' continuous service. Recently, two of us designed a modification to that level in which we think you would be interested.

We constructed several of the modified levels and our crew chiefs have now been using them for about one year and believe them to be a dramatic improvement. We have a patent application filed in the United States Patent Office and our attorney told us recently that the application had been approved.

We would be interested in selling our improvement to you for some sort of royalty since we are not in the tool-making field. We look forward to your reply.

Sincerely,

George L. Parrish

PLAINTIFF'S EXHIBIT

No. 2

SECTION H-3

From: Glen Eakin

To: Dave Horton

Sent: Monday, September 23, 1996 12:13 PM

Re:

I think the Parrish letter is worth following-up in view of the increased competition we are experiencing from imports. This could mean a new exclusive market for the United States. What should I offer them?

PLAINTIFF'S EXHIBIT

No. 3

SECTION H-4

ASSIGNMENT

WHEREAS WE, George L. Parrish and Charley A. Cooley of City of Columbus, County of Franklin and State of Ohio, are the inventors of certain inventions or improvements for which we have made application for Letters of Patent of the United States Entitled AN ADJUSTABLE PLUM AND LEVEL, filed March 20, 1996 and accorded Serial No. 452,879; and

WHEREAS Bullivant Tool, Inc., 135 South LaSalle Street, Chicago, Illinois 60603, a corporation of Illinois, is desirous of acquiring the entire right, title and interest in and to the said inventions or improvements and in and to the said application, and in, to and under any and all Letters Patent which may be granted on or as a result thereof in any and all countries:

NOW, THEREFORE, for One Dollar ($1.00) and valuable consideration, we have assigned, and do hereby assign, to Bullivant Tool, Inc. its successors, assigns and legal representatives ("Nominees") the entire right, title and interest in and to said inventions or improvements throughout the world and to said application and any and all Letters Patent, design patents and utility model patents which may be granted therefore, and all continuations, divisions, reissues, extensions and renewals thereof ("Letters Patent"); and we covenant that we have full right to convey the entire interest herein assigned, and that we have not executed and will not execute any agreement or do anything in conflict herewith;

And we further covenant and agree that we will, without delay, execute all such papers as may be necessary to perfect the title to said inventions or improvements, application and letters and Patent in Bullivant Tool, Inc., or it's Nominees, and we agree to communicate to said Bullivant Tool, Inc. or Nominees all known facts respecting said inventions or improvements, application and Letters Patent, to testify in any legal proceedings, to sign all lawful papers and generally to do all things necessary to aid Bullivant Tool, Inc., or its Nominees to obtain and enforce for their own benefit patent protection for said inventions or improvements in any and all countries, all at the expense, however, of Bullivant Tool, Inc., or its Nominees;

And we authorize Bullivant Tool, Inc., or its Nominees to file in our names or their own, an appropriate application for Letters Patent in all countries of the world, and we authorize the request to the Commissioner of Patents and Trademarks of the United States, and any proper official of any country, to issue to said Bullivant Tools, Inc., or its Nominees any and all Letters

PLAINTIFF'S EXHIBIT

No. 4

Patent for said Inventions or improvements, for their sole use, to the full end of the term for which such Letters Patent may be granted.

IN WITNESS WHEREOF we individually, have hereunto set our hand and seal.

George L. Parrish
George J. Parrish

Charles A. Cooley
Charley A. Cooley

State of Illinois)
)
County of Cook)

On this 20th day of March, 1997 before me personally came the above named individuals to me personally known and known to me to be the same individuals who executed the same of their own free will for the use and purposes therein set forth.

Donna M. Cosimini
Notary Public

My Commission Expires:

OFFICIAL SEAL
DONNA M COSIMINI
NOTARY PUBLIC, STATE OF ILLINOIS
MY COMMISSION EXPIRES:08/08/05

SECTION H-5

From: Glen Eakin

To: Dave Horton

Sent: Saturday, August 21, 1999 1:27 PM

Re:

While on vacation in Jellystone National Park, I had occasion to visit a hardware store. I was surprised to find on sale, the attached adjustable-length level, which is similar to our Model B-150A.

I have never heard of Pacific Machine Corporation before, but perhaps that's because my experience is limited to sales primarily in the Midwest. Perhaps you are aware of them. Should I contact them?

PLAINTIFF'S EXHIBIT

No. 5

SECTION H-6

Bullivant
Tool

September 27, 1999

Millard C. Pringle, President
Pacific Machine Corporation
230 Airport Way
Renton, Washington 98056

Re: U.S. Patent No. 5,624,056

Dear Mr. Pringle:

We have recently learned of your manufacture and sale of an adjustable-length level with a locking feature under the model designation PMC 20.

This letter is to notify you of the existence of our patent, a copy of which is enclosed. We ask that you immediately cease marketing this and all similar levels in the absence of a license from us.

I am today bringing this matter to the attention of our attorneys and you should expect to hear from them shortly.

Sincerely,

David W. Horton

David W. Horton, President

DWH/ss

PLAINTIFF'S
EXHIBIT

No. 6

SECTION H-7

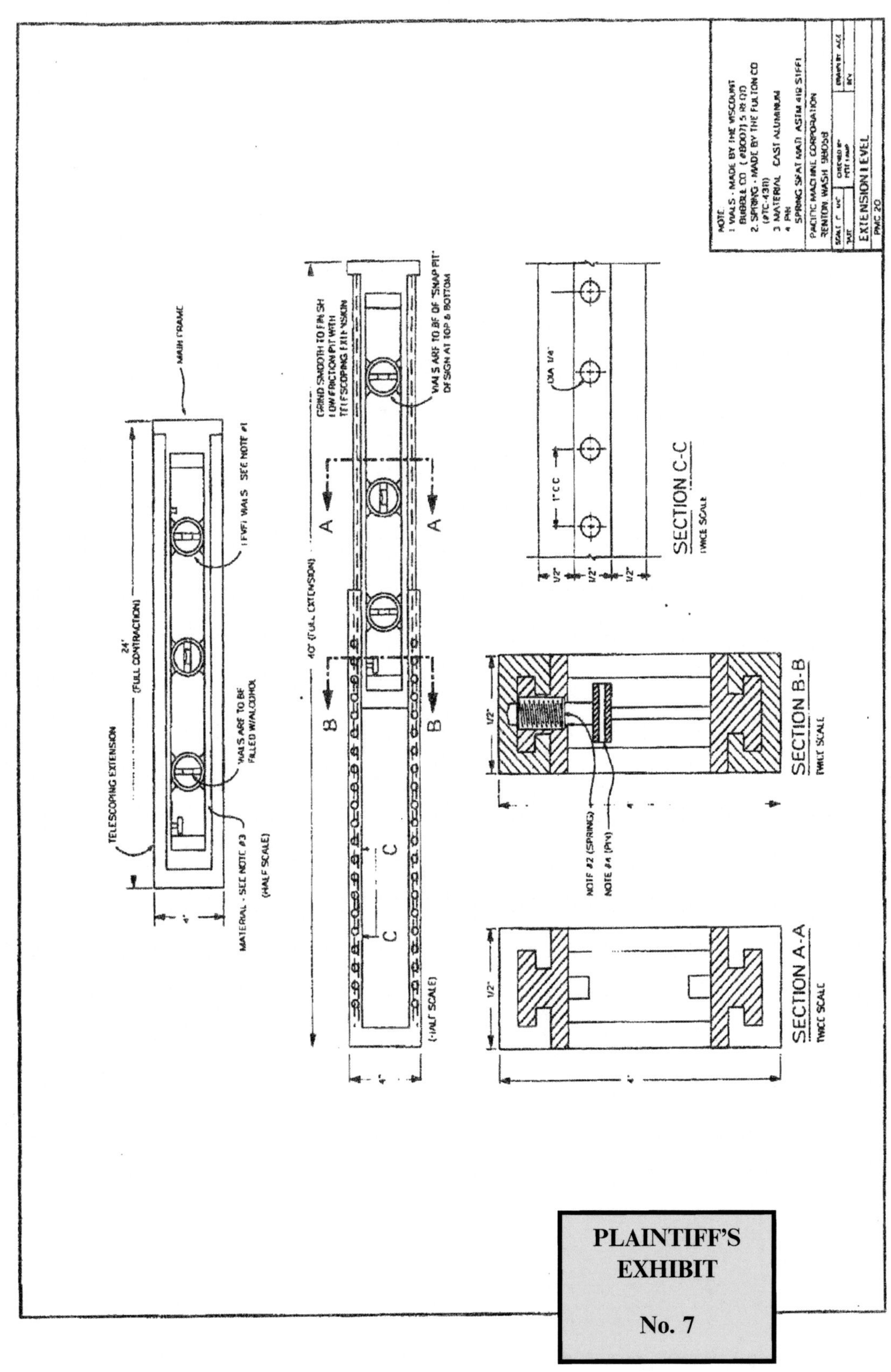

PLAINTIFF'S
EXHIBIT

No. 7

SECTION H-8

Physical Exhibit—An extensible level of Pacific Machine Corporation

SECTION H-9

MEMORANDUM TO FILE

FROM: S.N. Nellis

DATE: 11/22/95

RE: PMC – 20 Level

I visited James Smith, manager of Emerald Hardware in Seattle, Wash. last week to see if I could get him to place an order for the PMC-20 level. Smith expressed an interest in the level and said it reminded him of another product he had seen recently.

Smith indicated that a similar level had been given to him a few months ago by a guy who wanted to know whether his new level design would be attractive to customers. Apparently, the level got positive responses from Smith's customers.

Interestingly, Smith said that a designer from a small tool company in Renton, Wash. had visited his store in September and expressed interest in the level. The designer told Smith that he thought the level design was a winner.

Smith is interested in purchasing some of our levels, and will get back to me by Jan. 1.

PLAINTIFF'S EXHIBIT

No. 9

SECTION H-10

PLAINTIFF'S EXHIBIT
No. 10

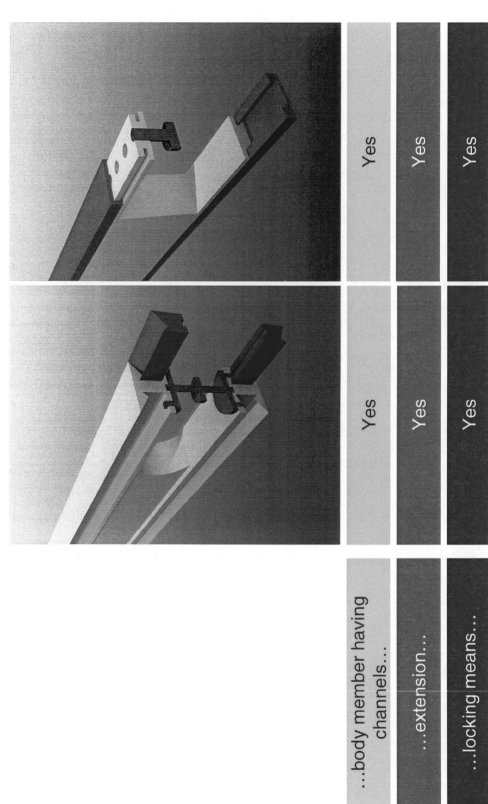

PMC Infringes

...body member having channels...	Yes	Yes
...extension...	Yes	Yes
...locking means...	Yes	Yes

SECTION H-11

PMC Infringes: *Willful and Deliberate*

PLAINTIFF'S EXHIBIT

No. 11

June 1996, PMC-20 went on sale

March 20, 1997, Parrish '056 assigned to Bullivant

April 22, 1997, Parrish '056 issued

August 21, 1999, Bullivant memo re: discovery of PMC-20

September 27, 1999, Bullivant notified PMC of infringement

April 20, 2004, Bullivant filed suit

1996 | 1997 | 1998 | 1999 | 2000 | 2001 | 2002 | 2003 | 2004 | 2005 | 2006

Section I

Exhibits Premarked by Defendant

(No Stipulations)

SECTION I-1

United States Patent [19]

L.J. Bullivant

[11] **Patent Number:** **5,351,524**

[45] **Date of Patent:** **April 30, 1991**

[54] **Extension Level**

[75] Inventors: **Lingham J. Bullivant**, Zion City, IL

[73] Assignee:

[21] Appl. No.: 1,189

[22] Filed: January 12, 1988

References Cited

U.S. PATENT DOCUMENTS

691,063	Leah	1/14/02
1,403,676	Eltag	1/17/22
1,413,056	Parrish et al.	4/16/22
1,450,904	Hunter	10/9/22
1,848,003	Chalupny	3/1/22
2,419,451	Keller	4/22/17

ABSTRACT

This invention relates to a hand instrument commonly used by carpenters, mechanics and others for truing surfaces in vertical or horizontal directions, and can be described as an extension device for obtaining greater accuracy in taking measurements by employing parts that are extensible. This invention allows a user to employ the leveling instrument using a shorter leveling device combined with an extension part to increase the accuracy obtained with a longer level. The shorter instrument is capable of collapsing so that it may be contained in a shorter tool case or cabinet. The invention also provides an extension level in which the extension part is accurately held with respect to the level indicating means to prevent lost motion and inaccuracies.

2 Claims, 4 drawings

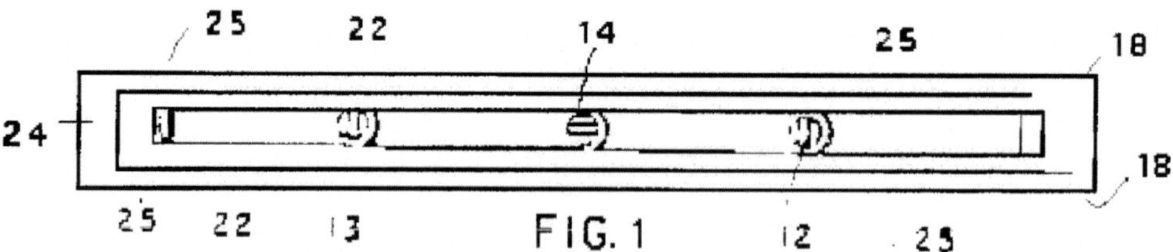

FIG. 1

DEFENDANT'S EXHIBIT

No. 1

U.S. Patent April 30, 1991 Sheet 1 of 1 **5,351,524**

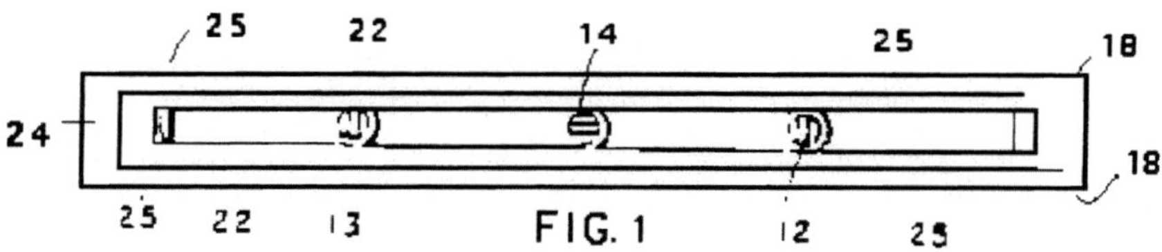

FIG. 1

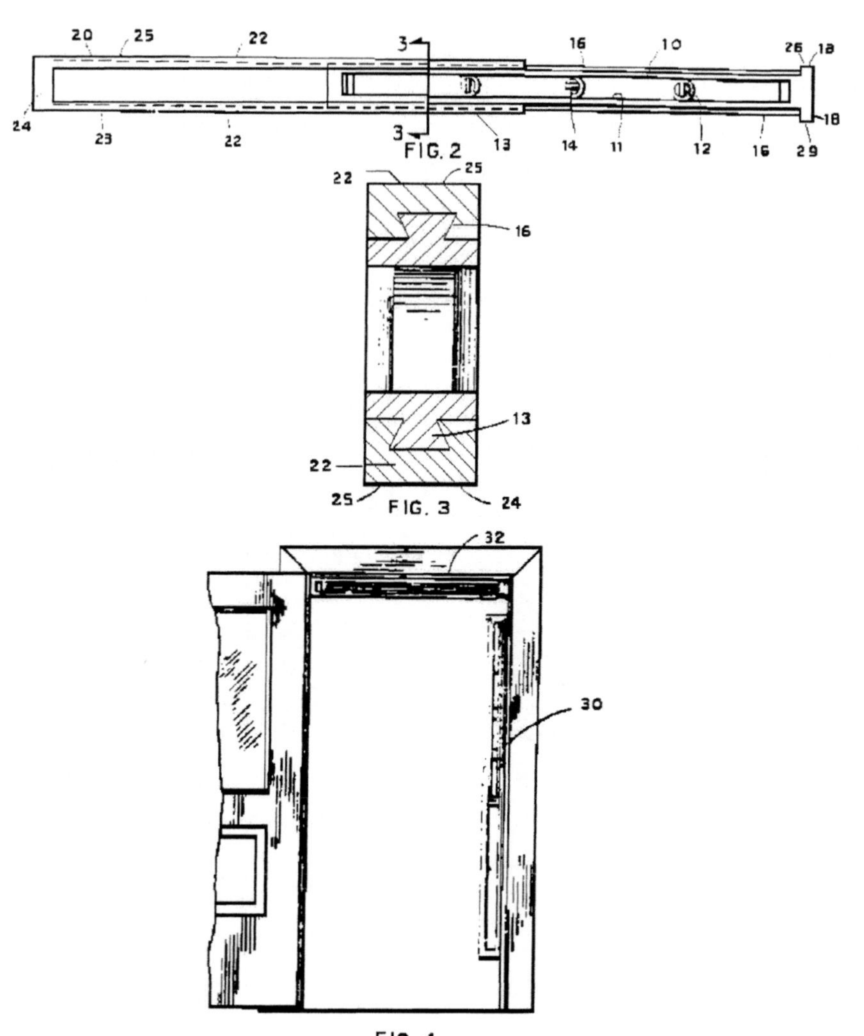

FIG. 2

FIG. 3

FIG. 4

5,351,524

1

FIELD OF THE INVENTION

BACKGROUND OF THE INVENTION

SUMMARY OF THE INVENTION

This invention relates in general to a hand instrument commonly used by carpenters, mechanics and others for truing surfaces in vertical or horizontal directions, and is more particularly described as an extension device of this kind for obtaining greater accuracy in such measurements by employing parts which are extensible.

An important object of the invention is to provide a level with an extension thereof by means of which greater accuracy can be obtained with the same leveling indicating parts.

A further object of the invention is to provide a leveling instrument in which a shorter leveling device may be combined with an extension part thereof to give the accuracy obtained with a longer level, the shorter instrument being collapsible so that it may be contained in a shorter tool case or cabinet.

Still a further objection of the invention is to provide an extension level in which the extension part is accurately held with respect to the level indicating means to prevent lost motion and inaccuracies.

DESCRIPTION OF THE FIGURES

Other objects of the invention will appear in the specification and will be apparent from the accompanying drawings in which.

Fig. 1 is a side elevation of an extension level in accordance with this invention in collapsed or closed position.

Fig. 2 shows the level of Fig. 1 in an extended position;

Fig. 3 is a transverse section take on the line 3—3 of Fig. 2; and

Fig. 4 shows the application of levels of this kind as applied to the top and side frames of a door.

DESCRIPTION OF THE PREFERRED EMBODIMENT

In using a level, it is desirable to have the instrument as long as possible to obtain greater accuracy; the shorter the level for measuring most surfaces, the less the accuracy for a carpenters' or tool makers' chest or cabinet. The practical limit in the length of a level is often determined by the size of the carrying case.

The present invention provides a means for practically doubling the accuracy of a level without increasing its size for carrying purposes; or stating it another way, the size of the level to obtain the same accuracy as now provided in such measurements may be cut substantially in half. By providing three or more similar extensible parts, the accuracy may be similarly increased or the size of the instrument correspondingly reduced.

Referring now more particularly to the drawings, a level of the type commonly used by carpenters and others comprises a frame 10 of metal, wood, or other suitable material having an interior space 11 in which are bubble levels 12 and 13 disposed in one direction and 14 disposed in a direction at right angles thereto.

The present invention includes side ribs 16 which are undercut or dovetail at both sides and preferably formed integral with the outer edges of the side frames. At one end of the level are projections 18 forming leveling extension which are project beyond the side ribs 16.

A telescoping extension 20 has side pieces 22 substantially as long as the frame 16 connected at one end by a crosspiece 24 preferably integral therewith. The inner edge of each side piece is

2

formed with an undercut or dovetailed grooves 24 adapted to fit closely but slidably upon one of the ribs 16 so that the extension may be applied to the level at the end opposite the projections 18 and telescoped upon the level until the crosspiece 24 engages the end of the level. Each outer surface 25 registers exactly with an outer surface 26 of the projection 18 and because of the dovetail connection between the ribs 16 and the grooves 24, these surfaces will be maintained in alignment throughout the movements of the extension in any position.

With this construction, the level in its collapsed or extended position may be applied to any surface and the engagement of the surface 25 and 28 at the same side in the extended position will increase the accuracy of leveling measurement of the instrument to the extent that the length of the instrument is increased. When applied to measure a somewhat length surface as a side frame 30 of a door opening, the level can be extended to its full length but when applied to a top piece 32, the level may be entirely collapsed or only partially extended. In each case, the contact surface 26 at one end of the level is accurately in alignment with the outer surface 26 of the same side of the instrument and contact with these two surfaces will serve to apply the instrument for leveling purposes.

Although the preferred construction has been described in detail, it should be regarded as an illustration or example of the structure and not as a limitation or restriction thereof, as many other constructions, combinations, and arrangements of the parts may be made without departing from the spirit and scope of the invention.

I claim:

1. An extension level, comprising a level frame having leveling devices mounted therein, projections at opposite side edges of one end of the frame, undercut ribs extending for the remainder of the side edges, extension rails connected by a crosspiece at the end opposite the frame projections, each rail having an inner undercut groove to fit the corresponding undercut rail and the two rails and the crosspiece fitting closely over the sides and one end of the level opposite the said projections, the outer edges of the rails and the projections of the level being held in alignment by the undercut ribs and grooves in all adjusted positions of the extension with respect to the level.

2. An extension level, comprising a level frame having leveling devices mounted therein and projections at opposite side edges of one end thereof, a U-shaped extension fitting over the other end of the frame at the side edges and end thereof and the outer edges flush with the outer edges of said projections, the respective outer and inner side edges of the frame and extension having interengaging tongue and groove slidable connections for holding the said outer edges flush with each other in all adjusted position of the extension.

SECTION I-2

5624056

SERIAL NUMBER (Series of 1987) 452879 | PATENT DATE APR 22 1997 | PATENT NUMBER 5624056

SERIAL NUMBER	FILING DATE	CLASS	SUBCLASS	GROUP ART UNIT	EXAMINER
452,879	03/20/96	22	365	243	Parker

APPLICANTS: GEORGE L. PARRISH AND CHARLEY A. COOLEY, BOTH OF COLUMBUS, OHIO

CONTINUING DATA*********************** 58
VERIFIED NONE

FOREIGN/PCT APPLICATIONS**********
VERIFIED NONE

DEFENDANT'S EXHIBIT No. 2

***** SMALL ENTITY *****

Foreign priority claimed ☐yes ☑no
35 USC 119 conditions met ☐yes ☑no

AS FILED	STATE OR COUNTRY	SHEETS DRWGS.	TOTAL CLAIMS	INDEP. CLAIMS	FILING FEE RECEIVED	ATTORNEY'S DOCKET NO.
		2.	1	1	$ 170.00	7961-1800

MORGAN & BROWNE, LLP
1400 K STREET, N.W.
WASHINGTON, DC 20006

ADJUSTABLE PLUMB AND LEVEL

U.S. DEPT. of COMM.-Pat. & TM Office — PTO-436L (rev. 10-78)

PARTS OF APPLICATION FILED SEPARATELY

NOTICE OF ALLOWANCE MAILED	PREPARED FOR ISSUE 01/07/97	CLAIMS ALLOWED
01/07/97	MICHAEL D. PARKER, Assistant Examiner; Nancy Noland, Docket Clerk	Total Claims: 1; Print Claim:

ISSUE FEE				DRAWING		
Amount Due	Date Paid			Sheets Drwg.	Figs. Drwg.	Print Fig.
$310.00	01/27/97	JOHN W. SHEPPERD PRIMARY EXAMINER GROUP 243	Primary Examiner	2	8	

ISSUE CLASSIFICATION		ISSUE BATCH NUMBER
Class	Subclass	
22	365	A38

Label Area

WARNING: The information disclosed herein may be restricted. Unauthorized disclosure may be prohibited by the United States Code Title 35, Sections 122, 181 and 368. Possession outside the U.S. Patent & Trademark Office is restricted to authorized employees and contractors only.

PTO-436

452879

APPROVED FOR LICENSE

INITIALS FEB 1 6 8 9 2 6

CONTENTS

Entered or Counted		Received or Mailed
	1. Application papers. #4 proto.	
	2. Rej. (3 mos.)	11/6/96
	3. Amdt A	11/20/96
	4. Notice of Allowability	1-7-97
	5. PTO GRANT APR 20 1997	
	6. Request for Cert. of correct.	7/8/97
	7. Cert. of correction Granted	9/9/97
	8.	
	9.	
	10.	
	11.	
	12.	
	13.	
	14.	
	15.	
	16.	
	17.	
	18.	
	19.	
	20.	
	21.	
	22.	
	23.	
	24.	
	25.	
	26.	
	27.	
	28.	
	29.	
	30.	
	31.	
	32.	

MAIL ROOM MAR 20 1996 54 PAT. & TRADEMARK OFF.

IN THE

UNITED STATES PATENT & TRADEMARK OFFICE

The Commissioner of Patents & Trademarks
Washington, D. C. 20231

DATE: MARCH 20, 1996

OUR CASE NO: 7961-1800

Sir:

Transmitted herewith for filing is the patent application (including specification, claims and declaration) of:

Inventor: GEORGE L. PARRISH, CHARLEY A. COOLEY

For: ADJUSTABLE PLUMB AND LEVEL

A. Enclosed are:

[X] Check No. 289 in the amount of $ 170.00 dated 3/20/96 is enclosed to cover the [X] filing fee or [ ] assignment recording fee.

[X] 2 sheets of drawing(s). [X] Formal [ ] Informal

[ ] An assignment of the invention to ______

[ ] A certified copy of a ______ application
[ ] Claim for priority under 35USC119.
[ ] Associate Power of Attorney.
[ ] Citation of Prior Art.
[ ] Preliminary Amendment.
[ ] Translation with Translator's Declaration.
[ ] Substitute specification with supporting declaration.

B. FILING FEE CALCULATION:

[ ] Before calculating the filing fee, please cancel claims ______.
[ ] After adding preliminary amendment claims ______.

SMALL ENTITY STATUS — AFFIDAVIT ATTACHED / LARGE BUSINESS RATE

For	Number Filed	Number Extra		Rate	Basic Fee $170	Rate	Basic Fee $340
Total Claims	1 -20	0	x	$6	170	$12	
Independent Claims	1 -3	0	x	$17	0.00	$34	
Multiple Dependency				$55		$110	
Total Filing Fee							
Assignment Recordal Fee					170.00		
				Total	$ 170.00	Total	$

C. SPECIAL INSTRUCTIONS:

[ ] Please charge our Deposit Account No. In the amount of $ ______.
A duplicate of this sheet is enclosed.

[ ] The Commissioner is hereby authorized to charge any fees which may be required, including, but not limited to payment of issue fees, or credit any overpayment to Account No. A duplicate copy of this sheet is enclosed. If this payment also requires a Petition, please construe this authorization to pay as the necessary Petition which is required to accompany the payment.

Michael Morgan
(Attorney)

MICHAEL MORGAN
REGISTRATION NO. 32,247

EXPRESS MAIL mailing label
No. ______
Date of Deposit ______
I hereby certify that this paper or fee is being deposited with the United States Postal Service "Express Mail Post Office to Addressee" service under 37 CFR 1.10 on the date indicated above and is addressed to the Commissioner of Patents and Trademarks, Washington, D.C. 20231. The person mailing this paper/fee is:
PRINT ______
SIGNATURE ______

SECTION I

PATENT

CERTIFICATE OF MAILING

I hereby certify that the attached Transmittal Letter in triplicate, Application entitled "Adjustable Plumb And Level", Two sheets of Formal Drawings, Declaration of Small Entity , Declaration and Power of Attorney, and Check for $170, are being deposited with the United States Postal Service as First Class Mail in an envelope addressed to the Commissioner of Patents and Trademarks, Washington, D.C. 20231, on March 20, 1996, with sufficient postage.

Michael Morgan
Registration No. 32,247

ADJUSTABLE PLUMB AND LEVEL

FIELD OF THE INVENTION

This invention relates to new and useful Improvements in Adjustable Plumbs and Levels.

SUMMARY OF THE INVENTION

This invention relates to plumbs and levels, and has for its object to provide a device of this character capable of being adjusted to the length desired.

Another object is to provide a device of this character including a movable extension capable of increasing the length of the plumb and level without destroying the shape thereof.

Another object is to provide a device of this character including a movable extension slidable on the support of the plumb and level glasses without interfering with the adjustment of the glasses.

A still further object of the invention is to provide a device of this character including a body member in which plumb and level glasses are adjustably mounted and wherein one end of the body member is movable away from and toward the body member of the medium of arms slidable in channels formed in opposite faces of the body member.

A still further object of the invention is to provide a device of this character including a body member in which plumb and level glasses are adjustably mounted and wherein one end of the body member is movable away from and toward the body member to the medium of arms slidable in channels formed in

SECTION I

opposite faces of the body member.

A still further object of the invention is to provide a device of this character wherein the body member is provided with means adapted to secure the extension in its adjusted position.

DESCRIPTION OF THE DRAWINGS

With these and other objects in view, the invention consists in the improved construction and arrangement of parts to be hereinafter more particularly described, fully claimed and illustrated in the accompanying drawings, in which:

Figure 1 is a side elevation of a plumb and level in its closed position,

Figure 2 is a side elevation of a plumb and level showing the extension in use,

Figure 3 is a section taken on the line 3—3 of Figure 1,

Figure 4 is a section taken on the line 4—4 of Figure 2,

Figure 5 is a perspective view of the extension,

Figure 6 is a plan view of the locking mechanism,

Figure 7 is a section taken on the line 7—7 of Figure 2, and

Figure 8 is a longitudinal sectional view of the structure shown in Figure 2.

DESCRIPTION OF THE PREFERRED EMBODIMENT

Referring to the drawings, 5 designates a body member formed from a single piece of material and including opposed work engaging faces 6i and 7, said faces being connected by mans of webs 8. The sides 9 and 10 of the body member adjacent the faces 5 and 6 are provided and channels 11, two channels being provided in each side. The channel extends upwardly and forwardly, and longitudinally of the body member 5. The outer wall 12 of the channel 11 is undercut to provide a channel 13, which serves to prevent lateral movement of an extension, the channel 13 being substantially V-shaped.

In order to increase the length of the body member 5, there is provided a novel extension, which consists of a body member or block 14 adapted to coincide with the end face of the body member and adapted to form one end of the body member. The block 14 is provided with a plurality of arms 15 and 16, one arm extending from each longitudinal corner or edge of the block. Each of the arms 15 has its face 15^a inclined inwardly and downwardly while the lower face 16^a of the arms 16 are inclined upwardly, the inner portions of said faces terminating below the inner edge thereof to provide a flange 17 and a channel 18. The flange 17 is adapted to be disposed in the channel 18, while the channel 18 is adapted to receive the ridge 19 formed at the junction of the channel 18 and the outer wall of the channel 11. The lower faces of the arms 15 and upper faces of the arms 16 are provided with grooves 21, said grooves extending longitudinally of the arms and terminating adjacent one end thereof to provide a stop. It will be noted that the lower faces of the arms 15 and upper faces of the arms 16 extend in parallel relation to the opposite faces of said arms. By this novel arrangement, the arms 15 and 16 are permitted to slide in the channels 11 longitudinally of the body member 5, lateral movement of said arms being prevented through the cooperation of the channel 13 and the flange 17, it being of course obvious that sufficient play is allowed to prevent the binding of the arms within the channels 11. 1

It will be noted that the outer face 22 of each arm is disposed closely adjacent the work engaging faces 6 and 7, and in right angular relation to said faces. The grooves 21 terminate adjacent the ends of the arms to prevent disengagement of the arms. The channels 11 and the arms, in view of their interlocking engagement, will eliminate the necessity of depending upon the block 14 to maintain the arms 15 and 16 in a true position when the extension is in use, and it is desired to obtain the exact level of work on which the device is used. The outer face 22 of each of the arms 15 is provided with a scale 23 which permits the operator to set the extension at the desired distance without the use of an additional or separate rule, it being also useful for other measuring purposes.

Projecting from the inner face of each of the work-engaging faces 6 and 7 is a socket 24, said sockets being disposed in opposed registering relation and between certain of the webs of the body member. These sockets are intended to receive the ends of a shaft 25, a knurled thumb nut 26 being secured to the intermediate portion of the shaft. The portion of the shaft on one side of the nut 26 is provided with right hand threads, while the remaining portion on the opposite side of the nut is provided with left hand threads. A locking plate 27, including a central threaded opening, is mounted on each threaded and portion of the shaft, the plates including fingers 28 adapted to extend through the inner wall of the channel into the grooves 21 of the arms 15, one finger being provided for each arm. It is of course obvious that when the shaft is rotated by means of the nut 26, in view of the right and left hand threads, the plate 27 will be moved toward or away from each other so as to cause the fingers 28 to extend into the grooves 21 and engage the arms 15. When the plates are moved away from each other toward the arms, the fingers come into binding engagement with the arms and thereby lock the same in their adjusted positions, movement of said plates toward each other releasing the arms to permit adjustment of the extension.

The intermediate portion of the body member 5 is provided with a channel 29, said channel having a plurality of openings 30. Disposed within the channel is a casing 31 having a pair of opposed ears 32 depending from the intermediate portion of the bottom of the casing. A socket member 33 is disposed between the ears 32, said socket member being interiorly threaded and having trunnions 34 projecting from one end thereof, said trunnions being journaled in the cars 32 to permit pivotal movement of the casing 31. A screw 35 is passed through one of the openings 30 into the socket member 33. Depending from the bottom of the casing 31 adjacent each end thereof is a threaded socket 36, each socket being adapted to receive a screw 37, which are passed through the remaining openings 30. By means of the screws 37 the casing 31 may be adjusted to various inclinations. Mounted within the casing 31 is a bubble or spirit level glass 38.

Disposed in spaced relation to the spirit level glass 38 is a plumb glass 39. This glass is adjustable similar to the glass 38 by means consisting of a casing 40 adapted to receive the glass 39, said casing being secured to the intermediate portion of a plate 41, the plate 41 having a pair of ears 42 depending from its lower intermediate portion. The plate 41 is disposed within the channel 43 formed in the body member 5. Said channel, similar to the channel 29, is provided with a plurality of openings 44. A socket member 45 similar to the socket member 33 is disposed beneath the plate for pivotally supporting the same. The ends of the plate are provided with sockets 46 adapted to receive screws 47 by means of which the plate 41 may be disposed in various inclined positions.

By this novel device, it is possible to increase the length of the body member without causing any portion of the extension to overlap the body member. In addition to this, by the novel formation of the channel 11 and the arms 15 and 16, the shape and accuracy of the body member is not disturbed even when the block 14 is disposed at the limit of its movement away from the body member 5. Furthermore, the arms 15 and 16 are disposed flush with the sides 9 and 10, no portion of the movable arms intersecting the work-engaging face of the body member, so that the extension may be operated even when the device is supported by the work, as the arms 15 and 16i do no t at any time engage the work. By a slight rotation of the shaft 215, the locking plates 17 are simultaneously moved to lock all of the arms of the extension in the desired adjusted position, the adjustable feature of the plumb and level glasses permitting the same to be maintained in various inclinations. The invention possesses every feature necessary to render a device of this character efficient and convenient for the user.

What is claimed is:

1. A plumb and level of the character described comprising a body member having channels, an extension disposed for sliding movement on the body member, and said extension having arms slidable in the channels of the body member.

ABSTRACT

ADJUSTABLE PLUMB AND LEVEL

This invention is an apparatus that relates to plumbs and levels and is capable of being adjusted to a length desired. The apparatus has a movable extension capable of increasing the length of the plumb and level without destroying its shape. It also has a movable extension slidable on the support of the plumb and level glasses without interfering with the adjustment of the glasses. The apparatus has a body member, that has the plumb and level glasses adjustably mounted and where one end of the body member is movable away from and toward the body member of the medium of arms slidable in channels formed in opposite faces of the body member. The body member is also capable of providing plumb and level glasses that are adjustably mounted and where one end of the body member is movable away from and toward the body member to the medium of arms slidable in channels formed in opposite faces of the body member.

COMBINED DEC[illegible]ATION AND POWER OF ATTORNEY [illegible] [illegible]RIGINAL APPLICATION	ATTORNEY DOCKET NO. 7961-1800

As a below named inventor, I hereby declare that:

My residence, post office address and citizenship are as stated below next to my name,

I believe I am the original, first and sole inventor (if only one name is listed below) or an original, first and joint inventor (if plural names are listed below) of the subject matter which is claimed and for which a patent is sought on the invention entitled ADJUSTABLE PLUMB AND LEVEL

the specification of which

(check one) ☒ is attached hereto.

☐ was filed on ____________

Application Serial No. ____________

and was amended on ____________
(if applicable)

I hereby state that I have reviewed and understand the contents of the above identified specification, including the claims, as amended by any amendment referred to above.

I acknowledge the duty to disclose information which is material to the examination of this application in accordance with Title 37, Code of Federal Regulations, §1.56 (a).

I hereby claim foreign priority benefits under Title 35, United States Code, §119 of any foreign application(s) for patent or inventor's certificate listed below and have also identified below any foreign application for patent or inventor's certificate having a filing date before that of the application on which priority is claimed:

Prior Foreign Application(s)

(Number)	(Country)	(Day/Month/Year Filed)	Priority Claimed Yes	Priority Claimed No
			☐	☒
			☐	☐
			☐	☐

I hereby claim the benefit under Title 35, United States Code, §120 of any United States application(s) listed below and, insofar as the subject matter of each of the claims of this application is not disclosed in the prior United States application in the manner provided by the first paragraph of Title 35, United States Code, §112, I acknowledge the duty to disclose material information as defined in Title 37, Code of Federal Regulations, §1.56(a) which occurred between the filing date of the prior application and the national or PCT international filing date of this application:

(Application Serial No.)	(Filing Date)	(Status) (patented, pending, abandoned)
N/A		

I hereby appoint the following attorney(s) and/or agent(s) to prosecute this application and to transact all business in the Patent and Trademark Office connected[illegible]

MICHAEL MORGAN
MORGAN & BROWNE, LLP, 1400 K STREET, N.W., WASHINGTON, DC 20006

Address all telephone calls to PLEASE SEE ABOVE at telephone 202-682-5000

Address all correspondence to PLEASE SEE ABOVE

I hereby declare that all statements [illegible] statements were made with the knowledge that willful false statements and the like so made are punishable by fine or imprisonment, or both, under Section 1001 of Title 18 of the United States Code and that such willful false statements may jeopardize the validity of the application or any patent issued thereon.

4/01/00

FULL NAME OF SOLE OR FIRST INVENTOR	INVENTOR'S SIGNATURE	DATE
GEORGE L. PARRISH	George L. Parrish	3/18/96
RESIDENCE: 600 WESTERVILLE ROAD, COLUMBUS, OHIO 43224		CITIZENSHIP: USA
POST OFFICE ADDRESS: SAME AS RESIDENCE		

FULL NAME OF SECOND JOINT INVENTOR, IF ANY	INVENTOR'S SIGNATURE	DATE
CHARLEY A. COOLEY	Charley A Cooley	3/19/96
RESIDENCE: 140 WHITETHORNE AVENUE, COLUMBUS, OHIO 43223		CITIZENSHIP: USA
POST OFFICE ADDRESS: SAME AS RESIDENCE		

FULL NAME OF THIRD JOINT INVENTOR, IF ANY	INVENTOR'S SIGNATURE	DATE
RESIDENCE		CITIZENSHIP
POST OFFICE ADDRESS		

SECTION I

Applicant or Patentee: GEORGE L. PARRISH ______ Attorney's Docket No.: 7961-1800
Serial or Patent No: ______
Filed or Issued: ______
For: ADJUSTABLE PLUMB AND LEVEL

VERIFIED STATEMENT (DECLARATION) CLAIMING SMALL ENTITY STATUS (37 CFR 1.9(f) and 1.27)

I. I hereby declare that I am making this verified statement to support a claim by ______ for small entity status for purposes of paying reduced fees under section 41(a) and (b) of Title 35, United States Code, with regard to the invention entitled ______

by inventor(s) ______
described in
( ) the specification filed herewith
( ) application serial no. ______, filed ______
( ) patent no. ______, issued ______

II. I hereby declare that I am:

(x) A. The above-named inventor and qualify as an independent inventor as defined in 37 CFR 1.9(c).

I have not assigned, granted, conveyed or licensed and am under no obligation under law to assign, grant, convey or license, any rights in the invention to any person who could not be classified as an independent inventor under 37 CFR 1.9(c) if that person had made the invention, or to any concern which would not qualify as a small business concern under 37 CFR 1.9(d) or a nonprofit organization under 37 CFR 1.9(e).

( ) B. A non-inventor making this verified statement to support a claim by ______. I hereby declare that I would qualify as an independent inventor as defined in Section II.A., above.

( ) C. An official empowered to act on behalf of a nonprofit organization as defined in 37 CFR 1.9(e) and identified below:
NAME OF ORGANIZATION ______
ADDRESS OF ORGANIZATION ______

TYPE OF ORGANIZATION:

( ) UNIVERSITY OR OTHER INSTITUTION OF HIGHER EDUCATION
( ) TAX EXEMPT UNDER INTERNAL REVENUE SERVICE CODE (26 USC 501(a) and 501(c) (3))
( ) NONPROFIT SCIENTIFIC OR EDUCATIONAL UNDER STATUTE OF STATE OF THE UNITED STATES OF AMERICA
(NAME OF STATE ______)
(CITATION OF STATUTE ______)
( ) WOULD QUALIFY AS TAX EXEMPT UNDER INTERNAL REVENUE SERVICE CODE (26 USC 501(a) and 501(c) (3) IF LOCATED IN THE UNITED STATES OF AMERICA
( ) WOULD QUALIFY AS NONPROFIT SCIENTIFIC OR EDUCATIONAL UNDER STATUTE OF STATE OF THE UNITED STATES OF AMERICA IF LOCATED IN THE UNITED STATES OF AMERICA
(NAME OF STATE ______)
(CITATION OF STATUTE ______)

( ) D. An owner or official of a small business concern empowered to act on behalf of the concern identified below:

NAME OF CONCERN ______________________________
ADDRESS OF CONCERN ______________________________
____

I hereby declare that the above identified small business concern qualifies as a small business concern as defined in 13 CFR 121.3-18, and reproduced in 37 CFR 1.9(d), in that the number of employees of the concern, including those of its affiliates, does not exceed 500 persons. For purposes of this statement, (1) the number of employees of the business concern is the average over the previous fiscal year of the concern of the persons employed on a full-time, part-time or temporary basis during each of the pay periods of the fiscal year, and (2) concerns are affiliates of each other when either, directly or indirectly, one concern controls or has the power to control the other, or a third party or parties controls or has the power to control both.

III. I hereby declare that rights in the above-identified invention under contract or law exist in or have been conveyed to and remain with the above-identified small entity.

If the rights held by the small entity are not exclusive, each individual, concern or organization having rights to the invention is listed below* and no rights to the invention are held by any person, other than the inventor, who could not qualify as a small business concern under 37 CFR 1.9(d) or by any concern which would not qualify as a small business concern under 37 CFR 1.9(d) or a nonprofit organization under 37 CFR 1.9(e). *NOTE: Separate verified statements are required from each named person, concern or organization having rights to the invention averring to their status as small entities. (37 CFR 1.27)

NAME ______________________________
ADDRESS ______________________________
( ) INDIVIDUAL ( ) SMALL BUSINESS CONCERN ( ) NONPROFIT ORGANIZATION

NAME ______________________________
ADDRESS ______________________________
( ) INDIVIDUAL ( ) SMALL BUSINESS CONCERN ( ) NONPROFIT ORGANIZATION

IV. I acknowledge the duty to file, in this application or patent, notification of any change in status resulting in loss of entitlement to small entity status prior to paying, or at the time of paying, the earliest of the issue fee or any maintenance fee due after the date on which status as a small entity is no longer appropriate. (37 CFR 1.28(b))

I hereby declare that all statements made herein of my own knowledge are true and that all statements made on information and belief are believed to be true; and further that these statements were made with the knowledge that willful false statements and the like so made are punishable by fine or imprisonment, or both, under section 1001 of Title 18 of the United States Code, and that such willful false statements may jeopardize the validity of the application, any patent issuing thereon, or any patent to which this verified statement is directed.

NAME OF PERSON SIGNING GEORGE L. PARRISH
TITLE IN ORGANIZATION INDEPENDENT INVENTOR
ADDRESS OF PERSON SIGNING
600 WESTERVILLE ROAD COLUMBUS, OHIO 43224
SIGNATURE George L. Parrish DATE 3/20/96

SECTION I

Applicant or Patentee: CHARLEY A. COOLEY ______ Attorney's Docket No.: 7961-1800
Serial or Patent No: ______
Filed or Issued: ______
For: ADJUSTABLE PLUMB AND LEVEL

VERIFIED STATEMENT (DECLARATION) CLAIMING SMALL ENTITY STATUS (37 CFR 1.9(f) and 1.27)

I. I hereby declare that I am making this verified statement to support a claim by ______ for small entity status for purposes of paying reduced fees under section 41(a) and (b) of Title 35, United States Code, with regard to the invention entitled ______
by inventor(s) ______
described in
( ) the specification filed herewith
( ) application serial no. ______, filed ______
( ) patent no. ______, issued ______

II. I hereby declare that I am:
(x) A. The above-named inventor and qualify as an independent inventor as defined in 37 CFR 1.9(c).

I have not assigned, granted, conveyed or licensed and am under no obligation under law to assign, grant, convey or license, any rights in the invention to any person who could not be classified as an independent inventor under 37 CFR 1.9(c) if that person had made the invention, or to any concern which would not qualify as a small business concern under 37 CFR 1.9(d) or a nonprofit organization under 37 CFR 1.9(e).

( ) B. A non-inventor making this verified statement to support a claim by ______. I hereby declare that I would qualify as an independent inventor as defined in Section II.A., above.

( ) C. An official empowered to act on behalf of a nonprofit organization as defined in 37 CFR 1.9(e) and identified below:
NAME OF ORGANIZATION ______
ADDRESS OF ORGANIZATION ______
______

TYPE OF ORGANIZATION:

( ) UNIVERSITY OR OTHER INSTITUTION OF HIGHER EDUCATION
( ) TAX EXEMPT UNDER INTERNAL REVENUE SERVICE CODE (26 USC 501(a) and 501(c)(3))
( ) NONPROFIT SCIENTIFIC OR EDUCATIONAL UNDER STATUTE OF STATE OF THE UNITED STATES OF AMERICA
(NAME OF STATE ______)
(CITATION OF STATUTE ______)
( ) WOULD QUALIFY AS TAX EXEMPT UNDER INTERNAL REVENUE SERVICE CODE (26 USC 501(a) and 501(c)(3) IF LOCATED IN THE UNITED STATES OF AMERICA
( ) WOULD QUALIFY AS NONPROFIT SCIENTIFIC OR EDUCATIONAL UNDER STATUTE OF STATE OF THE UNITED STATES OF AMERICA IF LOCATED IN THE UNITED STATES OF AMERICA
(NAME OF STATE ______)
(CITATION OF STATUTE ______)

( ) D. An owner or official of a small business concern empowered to act on behalf of the concern identified below:

NAME OF CONCERN ______________________________

ADDRESS OF CONCERN ______________________________

____

I hereby declare that the above identified small business concern qualifies as a small business concern as defined in 13 CFR 121.3-18, and reproduced in 37 CFR 1.9(d), in that the number of employees of the concern, including those of its affiliates, does not exceed 500 persons. For purposes of this statement, (1) the number of employees of the business concern is the average over the previous fiscal year of the concern of the persons employed on a full-time, part-time or temporary basis during each of the pay periods of the fiscal year, and (2) concerns are affiliates of each other when either, directly or indirectly, one concern controls or has the power to control the other, or a third party or parties controls or has the power to control both.

III. I hereby declare that rights in the above-identified invention under contract or law exist in or have been conveyed to and remain with the above-identified small entity.

If the rights held by the small entity are not exclusive, each individual, concern or organization having rights to the invention is listed below* and no rights to the invention are held by any person, other than the inventor, who could not qualify as a small business concern under 37 CFR 1.9(d) or by any concern which would not qualify as a small business concern under 37 CFR 1.9(d) or a nonprofit organization under 37 CFR 1.9(e). *NOTE: Separate verified statements are required from each named person, concern or organization having rights to the invention averring to their status as small entities. (37 CFR 1.27)

NAME ______________________________

ADDRESS ______________________________

( ) INDIVIDUAL ( ) SMALL BUSINESS CONCERN ( ) NONPROFIT ORGANIZATION

NAME ______________________________

ADDRESS ______________________________

( ) INDIVIDUAL ( ) SMALL BUSINESS CONCERN ( ) NONPROFIT ORGANIZATION

IV. I acknowledge the duty to file, in this application or patent, notification of any change in status resulting in loss of entitlement to small entity status prior to paying, or at the time of paying, the earliest of the issue fee or any maintenance fee due after the date on which status as a small entity is no longer appropriate. (37 CFR 1.28(b))

I hereby declare that all statements made herein of my own knowledge are true and that all statements made on information and belief are believed to be true; and further that these statements were made with the knowledge that willful false statements and the like so made are punishable by fine or imprisonment, or both, under section 1001 of Title 18 of the United States Code, and that such willful false statements may jeopardize the validity of the application, any patent issuing thereon, or any patent to which this verified statement is directed.

NAME OF PERSON SIGNING CHARLEY A. COOLEY

TITLE IN ORGANIZATION INDEPENDENT INVENTOR

ADDRESS OF PERSON SIGNING 140 WHITETHORNE AVENUE, COLUMBUS, OHIO 43223

SIGNATURE *Charley A Cooley* DATE 3/20/96

SECTION I

452879

Print of Drawing As Originally Filed

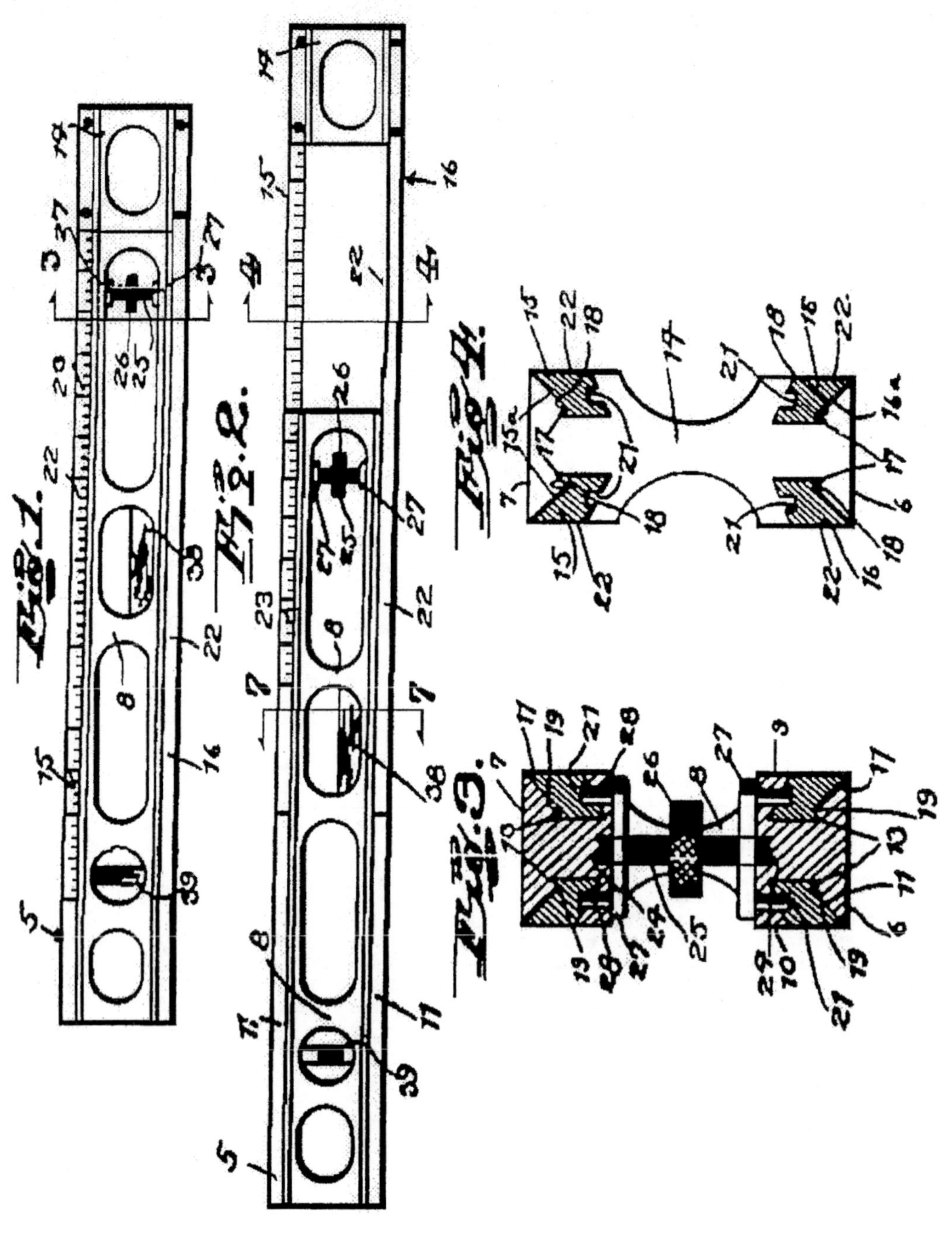

452879

Print of Drawing As Originally Filed

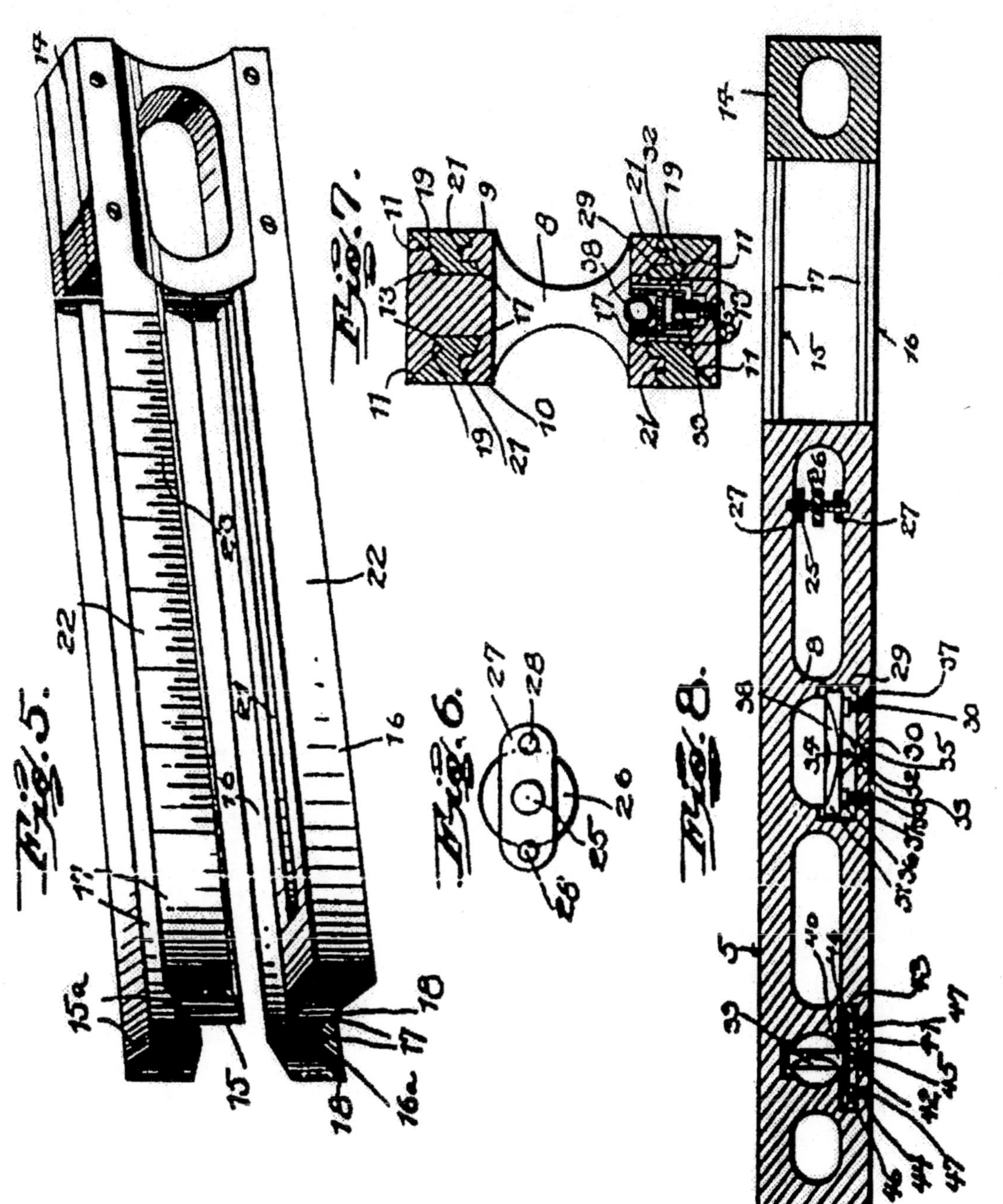

PATENT

IN THE
UNITED STATES PATENT AND TRADEMARK OFFICE

Art Unit 243
Examiner: M.D. PARKER

INVENTOR	GEORGE L. PARRISH, ET AL.
CASE	7961-1800
SERIAL NO.	452,879
FILED	MARCH 20, 1996
SUBJECT	ADJUSTABLE PLUMB AND LEVEL

THE COMMISSIONER OF PATENTS AND TRADEMARKS
WASHINGTON, D.C. 20231

SIR:

INFORMATION DISCLOSURE STATEMENT

Applicants submit the following reference pursuant to duty of disclosure under 37 CFR 1.56 with respect to the above-referenced patent application:

U.S. Patent No. 5,351,524, entitled "Extension Level"
by Bullivant

If it is felt for any reason that direct communication would help to further explain the relevance or pertinence of the enclosed reference, as well as the patentability of the invention, thereof, the Examiner is invited to call the undersigned at the below-listed number.

March 20, 1996

Respectfully submitted,

Michael Morgan

By: [signature]

Michael Morgan
Attorney for Applicant
Registration No. 32,247
Telephone: 202-682-5000

UNITED STATES DEPARTMENT OF COMMERCE
Patent and Trademark Office
Address: COMMISSIONER OF PATENTS AND TRADEMARKS
Washington, D.C. 20231

SERIAL NUMBER	FILING DATE	FIRST NAMED APPLICANT	ATTORNEY DOCKET NO.
452,879	03/20/96	PARRISH, GEORGE L.	7961-1800

MORGAN & BROWNE, LLP
1400 K STREET, N.W.
WASHINGTON, DC 20006

EXAMINER	
PARKER, M	
ART UNIT	PAPER NUMBER
243	2

DATE MAILED: 11/6/96

This is a communication from the examiner in charge of your application.

COMMISSIONER OF PATENTS AND TRADEMARKS

☒ This application has been examined ☐ Responsive to communication filed on ________ ☐ This action is made final.

A shortened statutory period for response to this action is set to expire 3 month(s), ~~days~~ from the date of this letter.
Failure to respond within the period for response will cause the application to become abandoned. 35 U.S.C. 133

Part I THE FOLLOWING ATTACHMENT(S) ARE PART OF THIS ACTION:

1. ☐ Notice of References Cited by Examiner, PTO-892.
2. ☐ Notice re Patent Drawing, PTO-948.
3. ☐ Notice of Art Cited by Applicant, PTO-1449
4. ☐ Notice of informal Patent Application, Form PTO-152
5. ☐ Information on How to Effect Drawing Changes, PTO-1474
6. ☐ ________

Part II SUMMARY OF ACTION

1. ☒ Claims 1 ________ are pending in the application.

   Of the above, claims ________ are withdrawn from consideration.

2. ☐ Claims ________ have been cancelled.
3. ☐ Claims ________ are allowed.
4. ☒ Claims 1 ________ are rejected.
5. ☐ Claims ________ are objected to.
6. ☐ Claims ________ are subject to restriction or election requirement.
7. ☐ This application has been filed with informal drawings which are acceptable for examination purposes until such time as allowable subject matter is indicated.
8. ☐ Allowable subject matter having been indicated, formal drawings are required in response to this Office action.
9. ☐ The corrected or substitute drawings have been received on ________. These drawings are ☐ acceptable; ☐ not acceptable (see explanation).
10. ☐ The ☐ proposed drawing correction and/or the ☐ proposed additional or substitute sheet(s) of drawings, filed on ________, has (have) been ☐ approved by the examiner. ☐ disapproved by the examiner (see explanation).
11. ☐ The proposed drawing correction, filed ________, has been ☐ approved. ☐ disapproved (see explanation). However, the Patent and Trademark Office no longer makes drawing changes. It is now applicant's responsibility to ensure that the drawings are corrected. Corrections MUST be effected in accordance with the instructions set forth on the attached letter "INFORMATION ON HOW TO EFFECT DRAWING CHANGES", PTO-1474.
12. ☐ Acknowledgment is made of the claim for priority under 35 U.S.C. 119. The certified copy has ☐ been received ☐ not been received ☐ been filed in parent application, serial no. ________; filed on ________.
13. ☐ Since this application appears to be in condition for allowance except for formal matters, prosecution as to the merits is closed in accordance with the practice under Ex parte Quayle, 1935 C.D. 11; 453 O.G. 213.
14. ☐ Other

PTOL-326 (Rev. 7-82) EXAMINER'S ACTION

Serial No. 452,879 -2-

Art Unit 243

1. Claim 1 is rejected under § 102(b) as anticipated by Bullivant patent. In regard to claim 1, Bullivant clearly discloses an extendable level with with a channel, a slidable extension and side pieces slidable in the channel.

2. Any inquiry concerning this communication or earlier communications from the examiner should be directed to Michael D. Parker whose telephone number is (703) 557-7744.

Any inquiry of a general nature, or relating to the status of this application, should be directed to the Group receptionist whose telephone number is (703) 557-3321.

M.D.PARKER:rf

703-557-7744

JOHN W. SHEPPERD
PRIMARY EXAMINER
GROUP 243

TO SEPARATE, H TOP AND BOTTOM EDGES, SNAP—APART AND …CARD CARBON

FORM PTO-892 (REV. 3-78)	U.S. DEPARTMENT OF COMMERCE PATENT AND TRADEMARK OFFICE	SERIAL NO.	GROUP ART UNIT	ATTACHMENT TO PAPER NUMBER
		452,879	243	2

NOTICE OF REFERENCES CITED

APPLICANT(S): PARRISH

U.S. PATENT DOCUMENTS

*		DOCUMENT NO.	DATE	NAME	CLASS	SUB-CLASS	FILING DATE IF APPROPRIATE
	A	5 3 5 1 5 2 4	1/88	BULLIVANT			
	B						
	C						
	D						
	E						
	F						
	G						
	H						
	I						
	J						
	K						

FOREIGN PATENT DOCUMENTS

*		DOCUMENT NO.	DATE	COUNTRY	NAME	CLASS	SUB-CLASS	PERTINENT SHTS. DWG.	PERTINENT PP. SPEC.
	L								
	M								
	N								
	O								
	P								
	Q								

OTHER REFERENCES (Including Author, Title, Date, Pertinent Pages, Etc.)

R	
S	
T	
U	

EXAMINER	DATE
	10/23/96

* A copy of this rererence is not being furnished with this office action. (See Manual of Patent Examining Procedure, section 707.05 (a).)

PATENT

IN THE
UNITED STATES PATENT AND TRADEMARK OFFICE

Art Unit 243
Examiner: M.D. PARKER

INVENTOR	GEORGE L. PARRISH, ET AL.
CASE	7961-1800
SERIAL NO.	452,879
FILED	MARCH 20, 1996
SUBJECT	ADJUSTABLE PLUMB AND LEVEL

THE COMMISSIONER OF PATENTS AND TRADEMARKS
WASHINGTON, D.C. 20231

SIR:

AMENDMENT A

In response to the Office Action mailed November 6, 1996, please amend the above-identified patent application, as follows:

IN THE CLAIMS

Please amend claim 1 as follows:

1. An extensible, non-overlapping [A] plumb and level of the character described comprising a body member having channels in the side faces thereof, an extension disposed for sliding movement on the body member, said extension having arms slidable in the channels of the body member, and locking means carried by the body member for frictional engagement with the arms to selectively prevent movement of the extension.

REMARKS

In response to the Office Action mailed on November 6, 1996, the Examiner's rejection under 35 USC 102 has been thoroughly considered. Claim 1, as presently amended, is believed to be patentable, and allowance is earnestly solicited.

It is respectfully submitted that Bullivant does not teach the present claimed combination. Bullivant is a typical extendable level including a frame with a movable extension. It doesn't provide the rigidity and strength achieved with the present invention as the extension moves. Further, Bullivant neither teaches nor suggests the combination of claimed features of an extensible, non-overlapping level having channels in the side faces and locking means carried by the body member for fricitional engagement with the arms to selectively prevent movement of the extension.

Therefore, Applicants submit that Claim 1 as amended is patentable, and allowance is respectfully requested.

If it is felt for any reason that direct communication would help to advance prosecution of this case to finality, the Examiner is invited to call the undersigned at the below-listed telephone number.

Respectfully submitted,

Michael Morgan

By: Michael Morgan

November 15, 1996

Michael Morgan
Attorney for Applicant
Registration No. 32,247
Telephone: 202-682-5000

SECTION I

PATENT

CERTIFICATE OF MAILING

I hereby certify that the attached Amendment A (3 pages), in connection with U.S. Patent Application Serial No. 452,879, entitled ADJUSTABLE PLUMB AND LEVEL (George Parrish, et al.), filed March 20, 1996, is being deposited with the United States Postal Service as First Class Mail in an envelope addressed to the Commissioner of Patents and Trademarks, Washington, D.C. 20231, on November 15, 1996, with sufficient postage.

Michael Morgan

UNITED STATE' 'PARTMENT OF COMMERCE
Patent and Trad. ·rk Office
Address: COMMISSIONER OF PATENTS AND TRADEMARKS
Washington, D.C. 20231

SERIAL NUMBER	FILING DATE	FIRST NAMED APPLICANT	ATTORNEY DOCKET NO.
452,879	03/20/96	PARRISH, GEORGE L.	7961-1800

MORGAN & BROWNE, LLP
1400 K STREET, N.W.
WASHINGTON, DC 20006

EXAMINER	
PARKER,M	
ART UNIT	PAPER NUMBER
243	4

DATE MAILED: 1/7/97

NOTICE OF ALLOWABILITY

PART I.

1. ☒ This communication is responsive to *the Amendment filed 11/15/96*.
2. ☑ All the claims being allowable, PROSECUTION ON THE MERITS IS (OR REMAINS) CLOSED in this application. If not included herewith (or previously mailed), a Notice Of Allowance And Issue Fee Due or other appropriate communication will be sent in due course.
3. ☑ The allowed claims are *1*.
4. ☐ The drawings filed on ____ are acceptable.
5. ☐ Acknowledgment is made of the claim for priority under 35 U.S.C. 119. The certified copy has [_] been received. [_] not been received. [_] been filed in parent application Serial No. ____, filed on ____.
6. ☐ Note the attached Examiner's Amendment.
7. ☐ Note the attached Examiner Interview Summary Record, PTOL-413.
8. ☐ Note the attached Examiner's Statement of Reasons for Allowance.
9. ☐ Note the attached NOTICE OF REFERENCES CITED, PTO-892.
10. ☐ Note the attached INFORMATION DISCLOSURE CITATION, PTO-1449.

PART II.

A SHORTENED STATUTORY PERIOD FOR RESPONSE to comply with the requirements noted below is set to EXPIRE THREE MONTHS FROM THE "DATE MAILED" indicated on this form. Failure to timely comply will result in the ABANDONMENT of this application. Extensions of time may be obtained under the provisions of 37 CFR 1.136(a).

1. ☐ Note the attached EXAMINER'S AMENDMENT or NOTICE OF INFORMAL APPLICATION, PTO-152, which discloses that the oath or declaration is deficient. A SUBSTITUTE OATH OR DECLARATION IS REQUIRED.
2. ☐ APPLICANT MUST MAKE THE DRAWING CHANGES INDICATED BELOW IN THE MANNER SET FORTH ON THE REVERSE SIDE OF THIS PAPER.
   a. ☐ Drawing informalities are indicated on the NOTICE RE PATENT DRAWINGS, PTO-948, attached hereto or to Paper No. ____. CORRECTION IS REQUIRED.
   b. ☐ The proposed drawing correction filed on ____ has been approved by the examiner. CORRECTION IS REQUIRED.
   c. ☐ Approved drawing corrections are described by the examiner in the attached EXAMINER'S AMENDMENT. CORRECTION IS REQUIRED.
   d. ☐ Formal drawings are now REQUIRED.

Any response to this letter should include in the upper right hand corner, the following information from the NOTICE OF ALLOWANCE AND ISSUE FEE DUE: ISSUE BATCH NUMBER, DATE OF THE NOTICE OF ALLOWANCE, AND SERIAL NUMBER.

Attachments:

- _ Examiner's Amendment
- _ Examiner Interview Summary Record, PTOL-413
- _ Reasons for Allowance
- _ Notice of References Cited, PTO-892
- _ Information Disclosure Citation, PTO-1449
- _ Notice of Informal Application, PTO-152
- _ Notice re Patent Drawings, PTO-948
- _ Listing of Bonded Draftsmen
- _ Other

NOTICE

ONLY OPTION 1.a) ON THE REVERSE MAY BE USED TO CORRECT DRAWINGS IF THE APPLICATION WAS FILED AFTER JANUARY 1, 1989; 37 CFR 1.85 (1097 O. G. 42).

Michael D. Parker
MICHAEL D. PARKER
(703) 557-7744

John W. Sheppard
JOHN W. SHEPPERD
PRIMARY EXAMINER
GROUP 243

PTOL-37 (REV. 2-85)

USCOMM-DC 85-3744

SECTION I

UNITED STATES DEPARTMENT OF COMMERCE
Patent and Trademark Office

Address: Box ISSUE FEE
COMMISSIONER OF PATENTS AND TRADEMARKS
Washington, D.C. 20231

MORGAN & BROWNE, LLP
1400 K STREET, N.W
WASHINGTON, DC 20006

NOTICE OF ALLOWANCE AND ISSUE FEE DUE

☒ Note attached communication from the Examiner
☐ This notice is issued in view of applicant's communication filed ______

SERIES CODE/SERIAL NO.	FILING DATE	TOTAL CLAIMS	EXAMINER AND GROUP ART UNIT		DATE MAILED
452,879	03/20/96	001	PARKER, M	243	1/7/97
First Named Applicant	PARRISH, GEORGE L.				

TITLE OF INVENTION: ADJUSTABLE PLUMB AND LEVEL

	ATTY'S DOCKET NO.	CLASS-SUBCLASS	BATCH NO.	APPLN. TYPE	SMALL ENTITY	FEE DUE	DATE DUE
	7961-1800	22-365.000	A38	UTILITY	YES	$310.00	3/7/97

THE APPLICATION IDENTIFIED ABOVE HAS BEEN EXAMINED AND IS ALLOWED FOR ISSUANCE AS A PATENT. PROSECUTION ON THE MERITS IS CLOSED.

THE ISSUE FEE MUST BE PAID WITHIN THREE MONTHS FROM THE MAILING DATE OF THIS NOTICE OR THIS APPLICATION SHALL BE REGARDED AS ABANDONED. THIS STATUTORY PERIOD CANNOT BE EXTENDED.

HOW TO RESPOND TO THIS NOTICE:

I. Review the SMALL ENTITY Status shown above.

If the SMALL ENTITY is shown as YES, verify your current SMALL ENTITY status:

A. If the Status is changed, pay twice the amount of the FEE DUE shown above and notify the Patent and Trademark Office of the change in status, or
B. If the Status is the same, pay the FEE DUE shown above.

If the SMALL ENTITY is shown as NO:

A. Pay FEE DUE shown above, or
B. File verified statement of Small Entity Status before, or with, payment of 1/2 the FEE DUE shown above.

II. Part B of this notice should be completed and returned to the Patent and Trademark Office (PTO) with your ISSUE FEE. Even if the ISSUE FEE has already been paid by a charge to deposit account, Part B should be completed and returned. If you are charging the ISSUE FEE to your deposit account, Part C of this notice should also be completed and returned.

III. All communications regarding this application must give series code (or filing date), serial number and batch number. Please direct all communications prior to issuance to Box ISSUE FEE unless advised to the contrary.

***IMPORTANT REMINDER:* Patents issuing on applications filed on or after Dec. 12, 1980 may require payment of maintenance fees.**

PATENT AND TRADEMARK OFFICE COPY

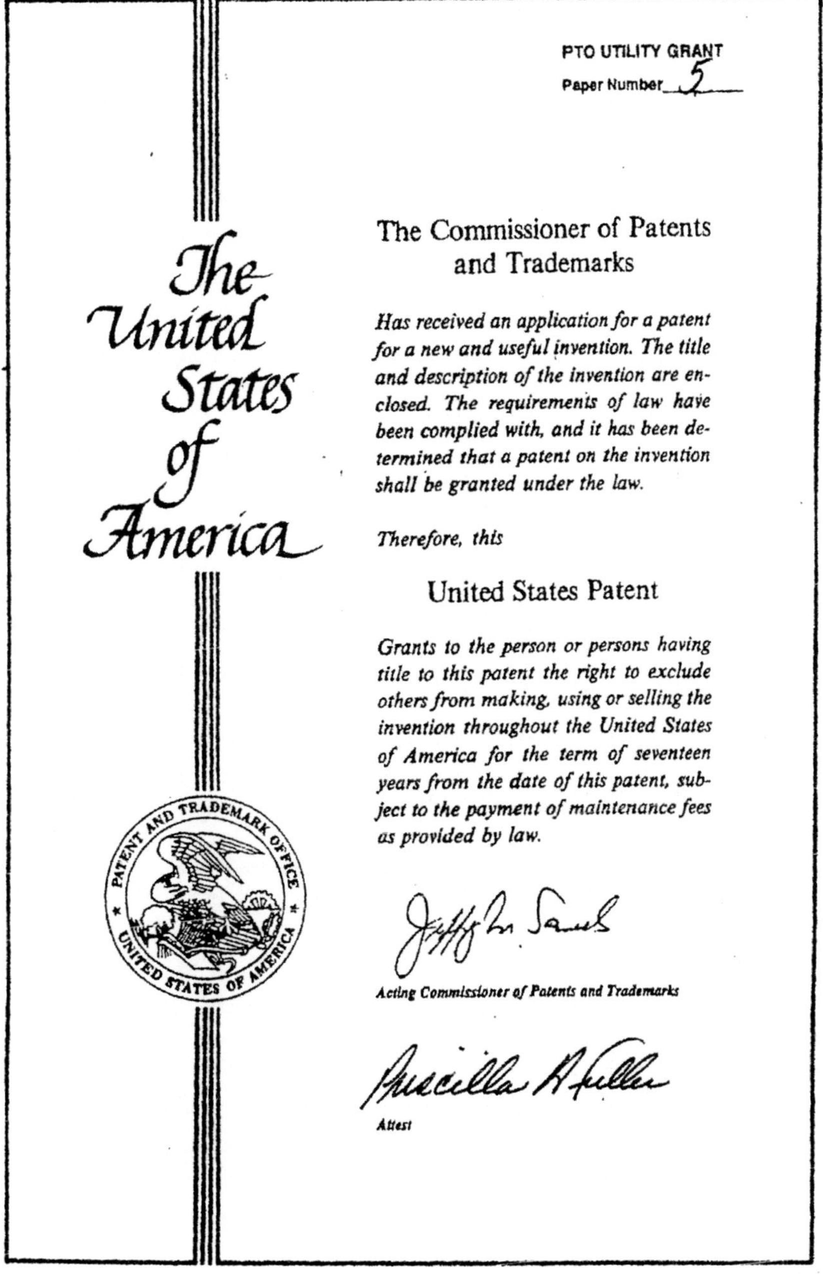

PTO UTILITY GRANT
Paper Number 5

The United States of America

The Commissioner of Patents and Trademarks

Has received an application for a patent for a new and useful invention. The title and description of the invention are enclosed. The requirements of law have been complied with, and it has been determined that a patent on the invention shall be granted under the law.

Therefore, this

United States Patent

Grants to the person or persons having title to this patent the right to exclude others from making, using or selling the invention throughout the United States of America for the term of seventeen years from the date of this patent, subject to the payment of maintenance fees as provided by law.

Acting Commissioner of Patents and Trademarks

Attest

United States Patent [19] | [11] **Patent Number:** **5,624,056**

Parrish et al. | [45] **Date of Patent:** **Apr. 22, 1997**

[54] **ADJUSTABLE PLUMB AND LEVEL**

[75] Inventors: **George L. Parrish; Charley A. Cooley**, all of Columbus, Ohio

[73] Assignee:

[21] Appl. No.: 452,879

[22] Filed: March 20, 1996

References Cited

U.S. PATENT DOCUMENTS

5,351,524 1/1960 Bullivant

ABSTRACT

This invention is an apparatus that relates to plumbs and levels and is capable of being adjusted to a length desired. The apparatus has a movable extension capable of increasing the length of the plumb and level without destroying its shape. It also has a movable extension slidable on the support of the plumb and level glasses without interfering with the adjustment of the glasses.

The apparatus has a body member, that has the plumb and level glasses adjustably mounted and where one end of the body member is movable away from and toward the body member of the medium of arms slidable in channels formed in opposite faces of the body member. The body member is also capable of providing plumb and level glasses that are adjustably mounted and where one end of the body member is movable away from and toward the body member to the medium of arms slidable in channels formed in opposite faces of the body member.

1 Claim, 8 drawings

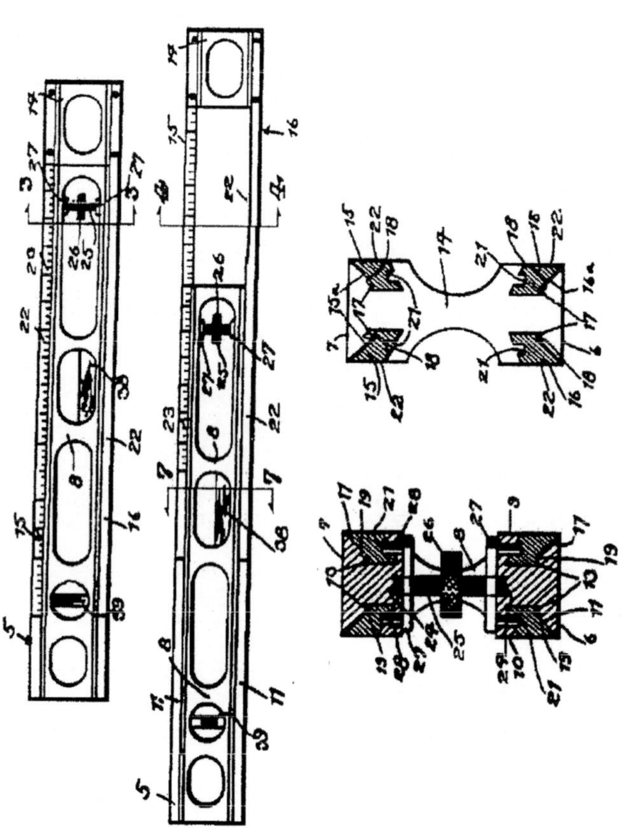

U.S. Patent April 22, 1997 Sheet 1 of 2 **5,624,056**

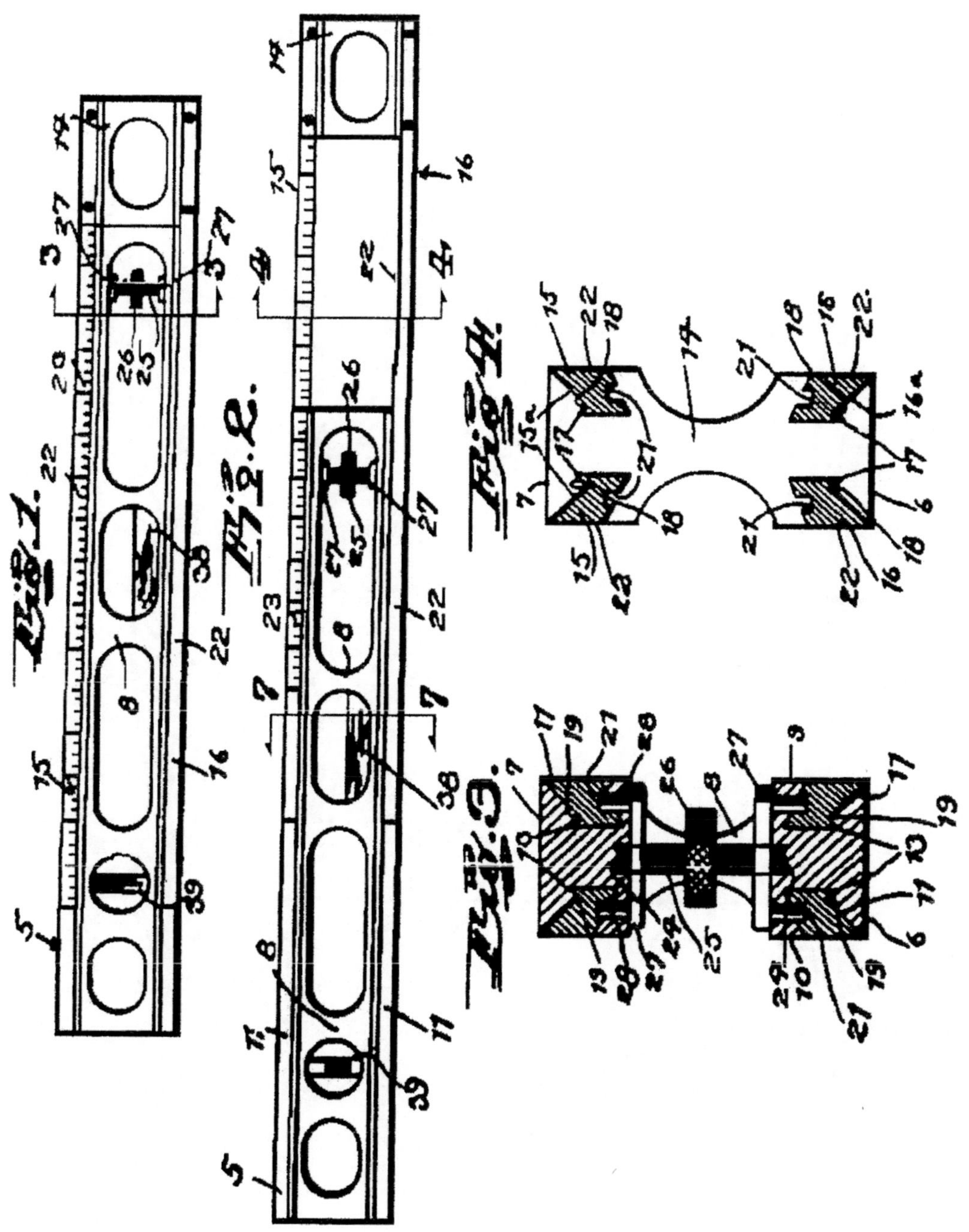

U.S. Patent April 22, 1997 Sheet 2 of 2 **5,624,056**

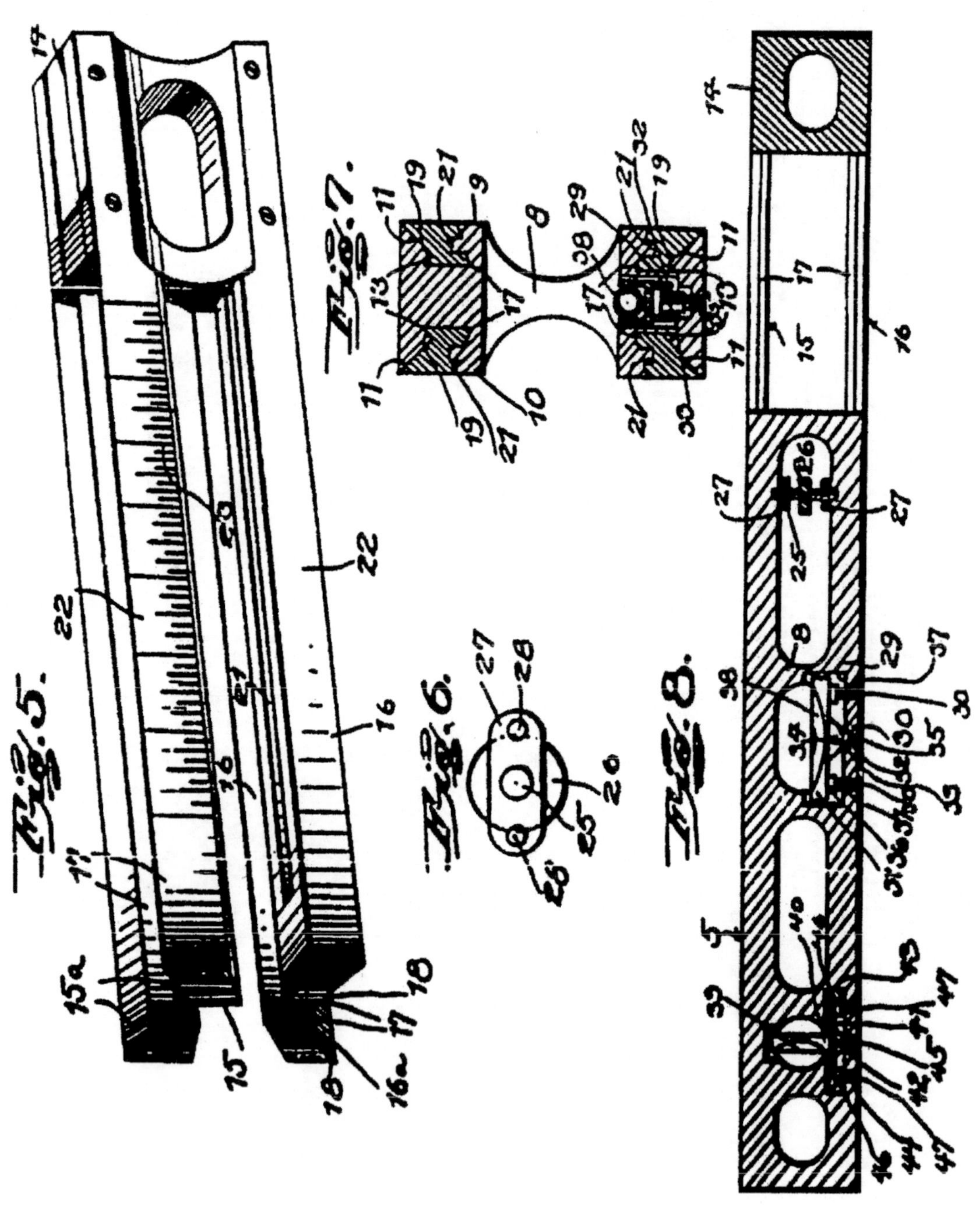

5,624,056

1

FIELD OF THE INVENTION

This invention relates to new and useful Improvements in Adjustable Plumbs and Levels.

SUMMARY OF THE INVENTION

This invention relates to plumbs and levels, and has for its object to provide a device of this character capable of being adjusted to the length desired.

Another object is to provide a device of this character including a movable extension capable of increasing the length of the plumb and level without destroying the shape thereof.

Another object is to provide a device of this character including a movable extension slidable on the support of the plumb and level glasses without interfering with the adjustment of the glasses.

A still further object of the invention is to provide a device of this character including a body member in which plumb and level glasses are adjustably mounted and wherein one end of the body member is movable away from and toward the body member of the medium of arms slidable in channels formed in opposite faces of the body member.

A still further object of the invention is to provide a device of this character including a body member in which plumb and level glasses are adjustably mounted and wherein one end of the body member is movable away from and toward the body member to the medium of arms slidable in channels formed in opposite faces of the body member.

A still further object of the invention is to provide a device of this character wherein the body member is provided with mans adapted to secure the extension in its adjusted position.

DESCRIPTION OF THE DRAWINGS

With these and other objects in view, the invention consists in the improved construction and arrangement of parts to be hereinafter more particularly described, fully claimed and illustrated in the accompanying drawings, in which:

Figure 1 is a side elevation of a plumb and level in its closed position,

Figure 2 is a side elevation of a plumb and level showing the extension in use,

Figure 3 is a section taken on the line 3—3 of Figure 1,

Figure 4 is a section taken on the line 4—4 of Figure 2,

Figure 5 is a perspective view of the extension,

Figure 6 is a plan view of the locking mechanism,

Figure 7 is a section taken on the line 7—7 of Figure 2, and

Figure 8 is a longitudinal sectional view of the structure shown in Figure 2.

DESCRIPTION OF THE PREFERRED EMBODIMENT

Referring to the drawings, 5 designates a body member formed from a single piece of material and including opposed work engaging faces 6i and 7, said faces being connected by mans of webs 8. The sides 9 and 10 of the body member adjacent the faces 5 and 6 are provided and channels 11, two channels being provided in each side. The channel extends upwardly and forwardly, and longitudinally of the body member 5. The outer wall 12 of the channel 11 is undercut to provide a channel 13, which serves to prevent lateral movement of an extension, the channel 13 being substantially V-shaped.

In order to increase the length of the body member 5,

2

there is provided a novel extension, which consists of a body member or block 14 adapted to coincide with the end face of the body member and adapted to form one end of the body member. The block 14 is provided with a plurality of arms 15 and 16, one arm extending from each longitudinal corner or edge of the block. Each of the arms 15 has its face 15[a] inclined inwardly and downwardly while the lower face 16[a] of the arms 16 are inclined upwardly, the inner portions of said faces terminating below the inner edge thereof to provide a flange 17 and a channel 18. The flange 17 is adapted to be disposed in the channel 18, while the channel 18 is adapted to receive the ridge 19 formed at the junction of the channel 18 and the outer wall of the channel 11. The lower faces of the arms 15 and upper faces of the arms 16 are provided with grooves 21, said grooves extending longitudinally of the arms and terminating adjacent one end thereof to provide a stop. It will be noted that the lower faces of the arms 15 and upper faces of the arms 16 extend in parallel relation to the opposite faces of said arms. By this novel arrangement, the arms 15 and 16 are permitted to slide in the channels 11 longitudinally of the body member 5, lateral movement of said arms being prevented through the cooperation of the channel 13 and the flange 17, it being of course obvious that sufficient play is allowed to prevent the binding of the arms within the channels 11. 1

It will be noted that the outer face 22 of each arm is disposed closely adjacent the work engaging faces 6 and 7, and in right angular relation to said faces. The grooves 21 terminate adjacent the ends of the arms to prevent disengagement of the arms. The channels 11 and the arms, in view of their interlocking

engagement, will eliminate the necessity of depending upon the block 14 to maintain the arms 15 and 16 in a true position when the extension is in use, and it is desired to obtain the exact level of work on which the device is used. The outer face 22 of each of the arms 15 is provided with a scale 23 which permits the operator to set the extension at the desired distance without the use of an additional or separate rule, it being also useful for other measuring purposes.

Projecting from the inner face of each of the work-engaging faces 6 and 7 is a socket 24, said sockets being disposed in opposed registering relation and between certain of the webs of the body member. These sockets are intended to receive the ends of a shaft 25, a knurled thumb nut 26 being secured to the intermediate portion of the shaft. The portion of the shaft on one side of the nut 26 is provided with right hand threads, while the remaining portion on the opposite side of the nut is provided with left hand threads. A locking plate 27, including a central threaded opening, is mounted on each threaded and portion of the shaft, the plates including fingers 28 adapted to extend through the inner wall of the channel into the grooves 21 of the arms 15, one finger being provided for each arm. It is of course obvious that when the shaft is rotated by means of the nut 26, in view of the right and left hand threads, the plate 27 will be moved toward or away from each other so as to cause the fingers 28 to extend into the grooves 21 and engage the arms 15. When the plates are moved away from each other toward the arms, the fingers come into binding engagement with the arms and thereby lock the same in their adjusted positions, movement of said plates toward each other releasing the arms to permit adjustment of the extension.

The intermediate portion of the body member 5 is provided with a channel 29, said channel having a plurality of openings 30. Disposed within the channel is a casing 31 having a pair of opposed ears 32 depending from the intermediate portion of the bottom of the casing. A socket member 33 is disposed between the ears 32, said socket member being interiorly threaded and having trunnions 34 projecting from one end thereof, said trunnions being journaled in the ears 32 to permit pivotal movement of the casing 31. A screw 35 is passed through one of the openings 30 into the socket member 33. Depending from the bottom of the casing 31 adjacent

SECTION I

5,624,056

3

each end thereof is a threaded socket 36, each socket being adapted to receive a screw 37, which are passed through the remaining openings 30. By means of the screws 37 the casing 31 may be adjusted to various inclinations. Mounted within the casing 31 is a bubble or spirit level glass 38.

Disposed in spaced relation to the spirit level glass 38 is a plumb glass 39. This glass is adjustable similar to the glass 38 by means consisting of a casing 40 adapted to receive the glass 39, said casing being secured to the intermediate portion of a plate 41, the plate 41 having a pair of ears 42 depending from its lower intermediate portion. The plate 41 is disposed within the channel 43 formed in the body member 5. Said channel, similar to the channel 29, is provided with a plurality of openings 44. A socket member 45 similar to the socket member 33 is disposed beneath the plate for pivotally supporting the same. The ends of the plate are provided with sockets 46 adapted to receive screws 47 by means of which the plate 41 may be disposed in various inclined positions.

By this novel device, it is possible to increase the length of the body member without causing any portion of the extension to overlap the body member. In addition to this, by the novel formation of the channel 11 and the arms 15 and 16, the shape and accuracy of the body member is not disturbed even

4

when the block 14 is disposed at the limit of its movement away from the body member 5. Furthermore, the arms 15 and 16 are disposed flush with the sides 9 and 10, no portion of the movable arms intersecting the work-engaging face of the body member, so that the extension may be operated even when the device is supported by the work, as the arms 15 and 16i do no t at any time engage the work. By a slight rotation of the shaft 215, the locking plates 17 are simultaneously moved to lock all of the arms of the extension in the desired adjusted position, the adjustable feature of the plumb and level glasses permitting the same to be maintained in various inclinations. The invention possesses every feature necessary to render a device of this character efficient and convenient for the user.

What is claimed is:

1. An extensible, non-overlapping plumb and level of the character described comprising a body member having channels in the side faces thereof, an extension disposed for sliding movement on the body member, said extension having arms slidable in the channels of the body member, and locking means carried by the body member for frictional engagement with the arms to selectively prevent movement of the extension.

SECTION I-3

From: Sue Parrish

To: Charley Cooley

Sent: Friday, December 10, 2004 3:10 PM

Subject:

Dear Charley:

When I heard that there was some sort of lawsuit involving the level which you and George patented, I recalled recently seeing this letter in some of George's personal records. It took me some time to find it since the letter was not in with the rest of the patent stuff or even with his other legal papers and files.

The letter is from his grandfather for whom George was named. I think you may have met him in 1983. He was a little eccentric, but a nice old gentleman. I hope this letter is of some help.

Sincerely,

Sue

DEFENDANT'S EXHIBIT

No. 3

SECTION I-4

Golden Years Mobile Park
#16A
Sarasota, Fla.
October 7 1979

Dear Georgie,

I understand from Millicent that you have now returned home from Germany and are now out of the Army. We are all happy to have you back with us. Since you were in the Engineering Corps and did not see action. It could not have been any worse for you boys than it was for us at Iwo Jima. I remember the time our company had been practically wiped out. I held a machine gun position surrounded by the enemy, and managed to hold off almost an entire enemy battalion for at least two hours until reinforcements arrived. Truly one of my bravest hours – escaped without a scratch too!

Enough of old war stories. Millicent tells me that you managed to complete high school before going into the Army and have decided to forego college for now and instead try your hand in the construction trades since you liked the work in the Engineering Corps but didn't want to make the Army a career. I know your father will be proud to have you join him in the family business. I have a lot of faith in your abilities.

DEFENDANT'S EXHIBIT

No. 4

- 2 -

Perhaps in your spare time you might want to work on an old idea I had for an extendable length level. I can't seem to find the old thing in my tools although I used it on the job for several years back in the early 30's. I think I may have sold it during the depression or it may have just ended up as firewood one winter when we lived in Cleveland since we had very little money back then. The family firm has since done very well and I'm happy to have you be a part of it.

I have drawn two figures in the enclosed drawing showing how the old level worked. The metal casings were slidable on the wooden stock and could be locked in any positions by tightening the thumbscrews. The scale (dial) was hidden and protected by the sleeves when in their closed positions. The scale was used in conjunction with a line and plumb bob to read the angle. Of course today one would probably substitute a spirit bubble indicator or two.

Well, even if you don't ever do anything with it, I thought you might get a kick out of seeing it.

Millicent and I look forward to seeing you and the family for Christmas. It will be nice to have everyone together again for the

-3-

first time in four years. Maybe we can exchange a few army stories.

Love,
Grandpa

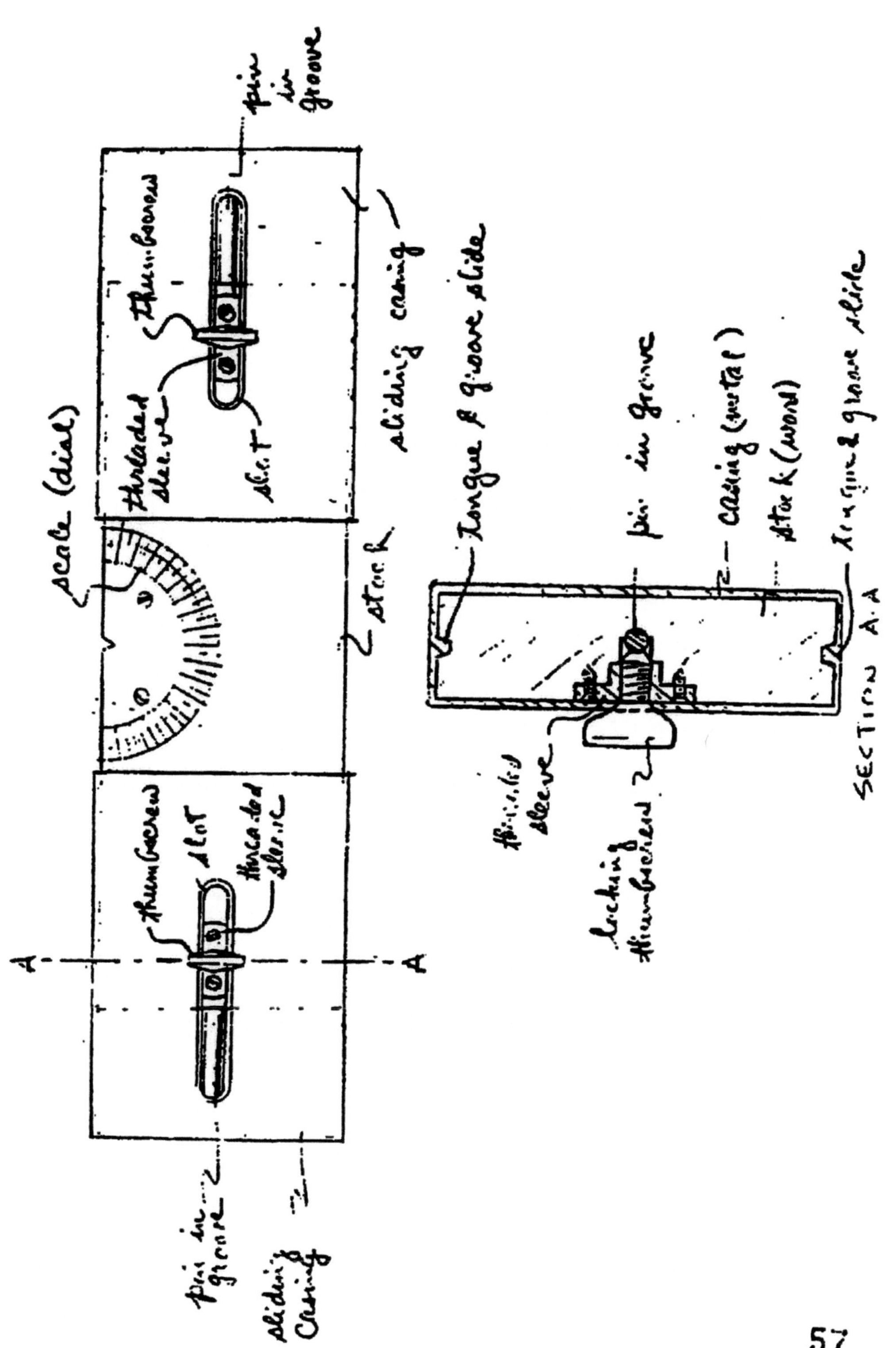
scale (dial)
stock
threaded sleeve
slot
thumbscrew
pin in groove
sliding casing
tongue & groove slide
casing (metal)
stock (wood)
locking thumbscrew
SECTION A-A
A
A

SECTION I-5

PACIFIC MACHINE CORPORATION
Renton Washington 98055

MEMORANDUM

TO: S.N. Nellis
A.C. Edgar
P.T. Lamp

Re: Patent Problem with PMC-20

FROM: M.C. Pringle

DATE: October 18, 1999

We have just received the attached letter from Bullivant Tool, Inc. accusing us of patent infringement. Our attorney has asked that we review our files by next Thursday and gather all the information we have on the design and development of the PMC-20 and on any other extension levels known to us at this time.

We will meet with him on Thursday in our conference room at 9:30 A.M. to review the situation. Be prepared!

M. C. P.

DEFENDANT'S EXHIBIT

No. 5

SECTION I-6

PACIFIC MACHINE CORPORATION
Renton Washington 98055

MEMORANDUM

TO: S.N. Nellis
P.T. Lamp

Re: Patent Problem with PMC-20

FROM: A.C. Edgar

DATE: November 14, 1995

The design of the new locking extensible level is to the point that we should look into getting a patent. What is the company patent policy? If none exists, I suggest that one be adopted.

Attached is a copy of the finished design drawing.

ACE.

SECTION I

DEFENDANT'S EXHIBIT

No. 6

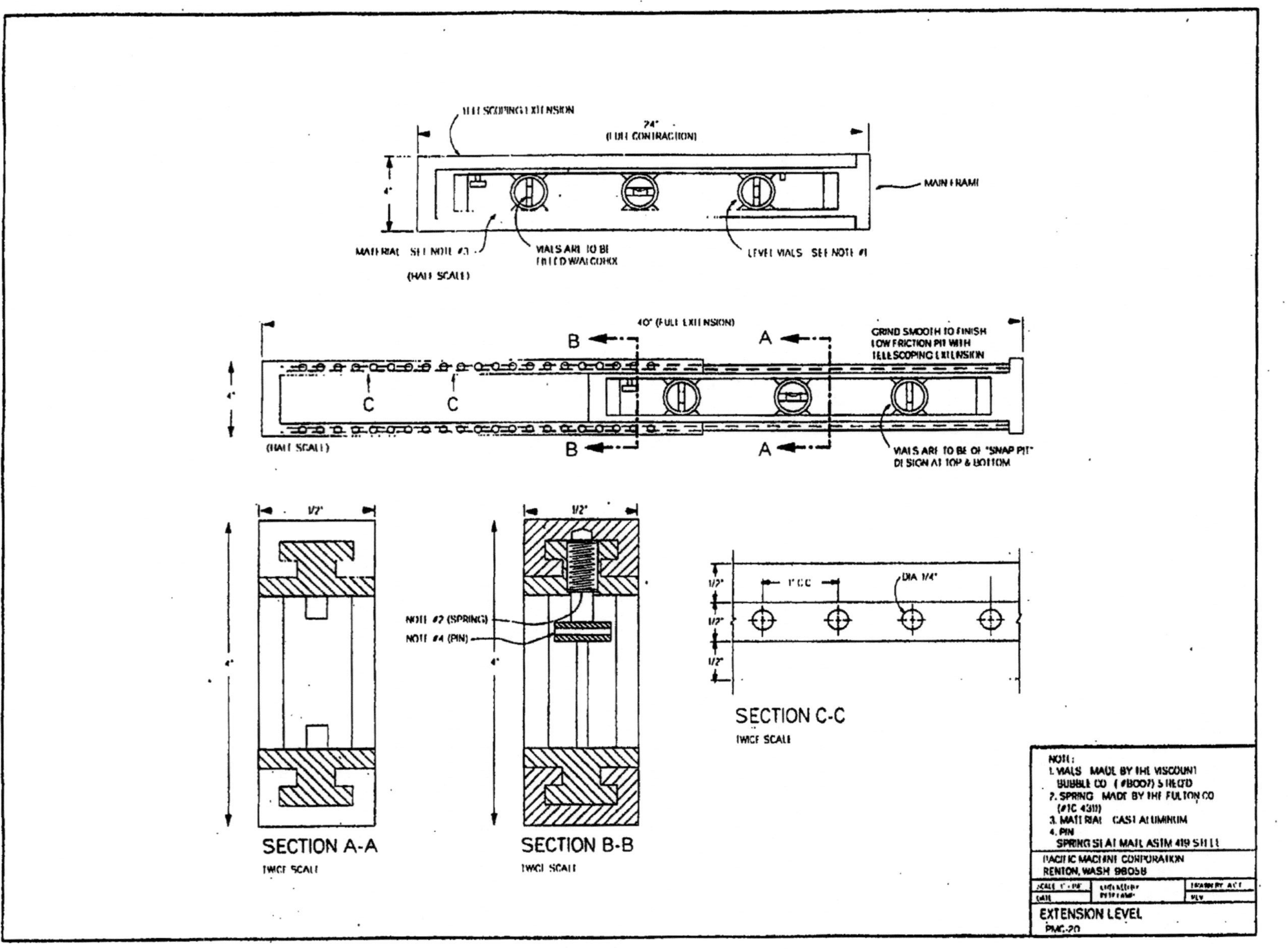
TELESCOPING EXTENSION
24"
(FULL CONTRACTION)
MAIN FRAME
4"
MATERIAL SEE NOTE #3
VIALS ARE TO BE
LEVEL VIALS SEE NOTE #1
(HALF SCALE)
40" (FULL EXTENSION)
GRIND SMOOTH TO FINISH
LOW FRICTION FIT WITH
TELESCOPING EXTENSION
B
A
C
C
(HALF SCALE)
VIALS ARE TO BE OF "SNAP FIT"
DESIGN AT TOP & BOTTOM
1/2"
NOTE #2 (SPRING)
NOTE #4 (PIN)
1" C C
DIA 1/4"
SECTION C-C
TWICE SCALE
SECTION A-A
TWICE SCALE
SECTION B-B
TWICE SCALE
NOTE:
1. VIALS MADE BY THE VISCOUNT BUBBLE CO (#B007) 5 REQ'D
2. SPRING MADE BY THE FULTON CO (#C 4311)
3. MATERIAL CAST ALUMINUM
4. PIN
SPRING STEAT MATL ASTM 419 STEEL
PACIFIC MACHINE CORPORATION
RENTON, WASH 98058
EXTENSION LEVEL
PMC-20

SECTION I-7

PACIFIC MACHINE CORPORATION
Renton Washington 98055

MEMORANDUM

TO: A.C. Edgar
P.T. Lamp

Re: Patents

FROM: S.N. Nellis

DATE: November 15, 1995

Due to the present economic situation of the company, we have a policy of not filing for patents. We hope that with the addition of new successful products due to your efforts, we will be able to afford the expenses involved.

Stu

DEFENDANT'S EXHIBIT

No. 7

SECTION I-8

PACIFIC MACHINE CORPORATION
Renton Washington 98055

MEMORANDUM

TO: M.C. Pringle
A.C. Edgar

Re: PMC-20

FROM: S.N. Nellis

DATE: May 24, 1996

The planning and engineering are about to bear fruit. We will start our sales campaign next Monday on the new PMC-20 Extension Level. We are anticipating orders of about 3,000 units by the end of June.

I am informed that we have on hand a 700-unit stock (the initial 300 being given away as sales promotion items). Pete tells me that production should be about 500 per week by the end of June although it is only at 300 per week now.

Stu

DEFENDANT'S EXHIBIT

No. 8

SECTION I-9

PACIFIC MACHINE CORPORATION
Renton Washington 98055

MEMORANDUM

TO: M.C. Pringle Re: Bullivant vs. PMC

FROM: S.N. Nellis DATE: January 7, 2005

I have asked C.W. Woods of our Data Processing Department for the relevant business information from our computerized records concerning our growth and expansion during the years 1999-2004. I have summarized this information as follows:

For Year Ending	Employment	Advertising and Sales. Prom. ($000)	Sales ($000)	Plant & Equip. – Additions ($000)
1999	150	92	950	15
2000	195	110	1,360	57
2001	210	173	1,923	64
2002	240	241	2,703	127
2003	247	339	3,456	209
2004	260	423	4,950	870

DEFENDANT'S EXHIBIT

No. 9

SECTION I-10

PARRISH CONSTRUCTION COMPANY

MEMORANDUM

TO: George Parrish

FROM: Charley Cooley

DATE: October 5, 1995

RE: Construction Materials for New Level Design

After our discussion last week regarding what material to use in manufacturing our new level commercially, I did some research on the matter and have a couple of comments.

First, if we want to make the level lightweight, but very durable, we should use aluminum. Aluminum may provide the necessary friction we need between the locking mechanism and the arms, but we may consider that using some additional coating substance in the channels might be necessary. Maybe a carbon coating would do the job.

Second, if we want to make the level heavier, we should use carbonated steel. This will also provide the necessary frictional contact force between the lock and the arms without the need for any additional coating.

I think we should use steel because the levels will appear more durable if they weigh more, and therefore will be more appealing to construction types. The extra weight may also increase accuracy. We may want to consult with some of the crews that are currently using our prototypes to see if they have a preference.

DEFENDANT'S
EXHIBIT

No. 10

SECTION I-11

From: Nelsonn, J.

To: Eaken, G.

Sent: Tuesday, August 10, 2004 2:45 PM

Re: Potential Litigation Issue

In reviewing the Parrish files, I found a copy of a memo from Cooley to Parrish regarding materials that may be used to construct the level. It mentions the possibility of using aluminum or steel. Parrish favored steel because it was heavier, might improve the functioning of the level, and might be more appealing to "construction types."

I think that there's some sort of duty to disclose the best way of making your invention when you file a patent application. I suppose that PMC could argue that Cooley and Parrish had some obligation to tell the Patent Office about the two preferred materials from which to manufacture the level, and the benefits of using one material or the other. However, the memo only gives Parrish's opinion, not actual facts about the operation of the level. I can't find anything to suggest that they had confirmed Parrish's guesses about the benefits of the two materials. If they didn't know which material was best, they couldn't have violated their duty to the Patent Office.

Just thought I'd let you know about this in case you hear anything from PMC. They got a copy of Parrish's files, so you might.

DEFENDANT'S EXHIBIT

No. 11

SECTION I-12

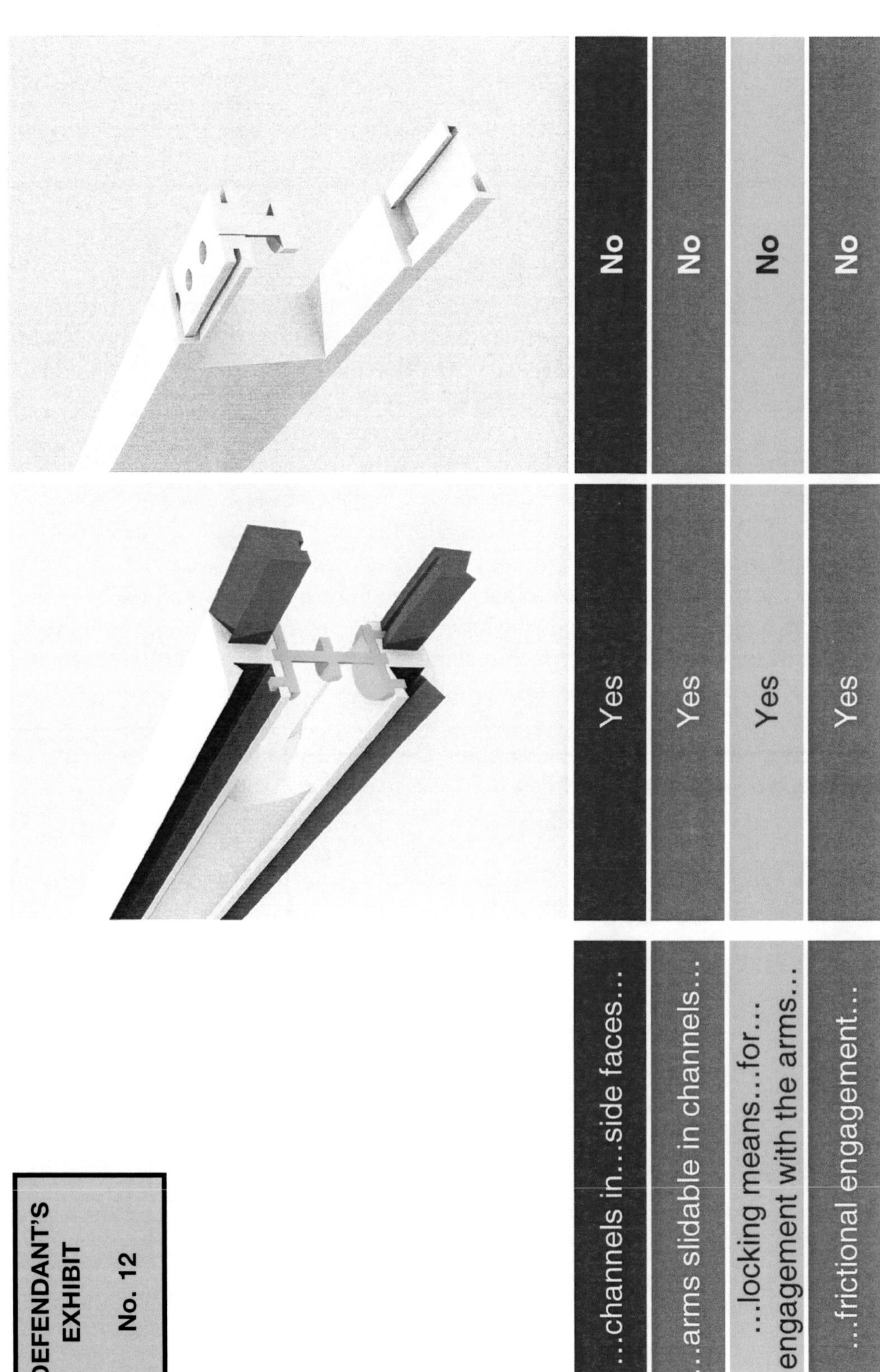
PMC Does NOT Infringe
DEFENDANT'S
EXHIBIT
No. 12
…channels in…side faces…
…arms slidable in channels…
…locking means…for…
engagement with the arms…
…frictional engagement…
Yes
Yes
Yes
Yes
No
No
No
No

SECTION I-13

Parrish '056 Obvious

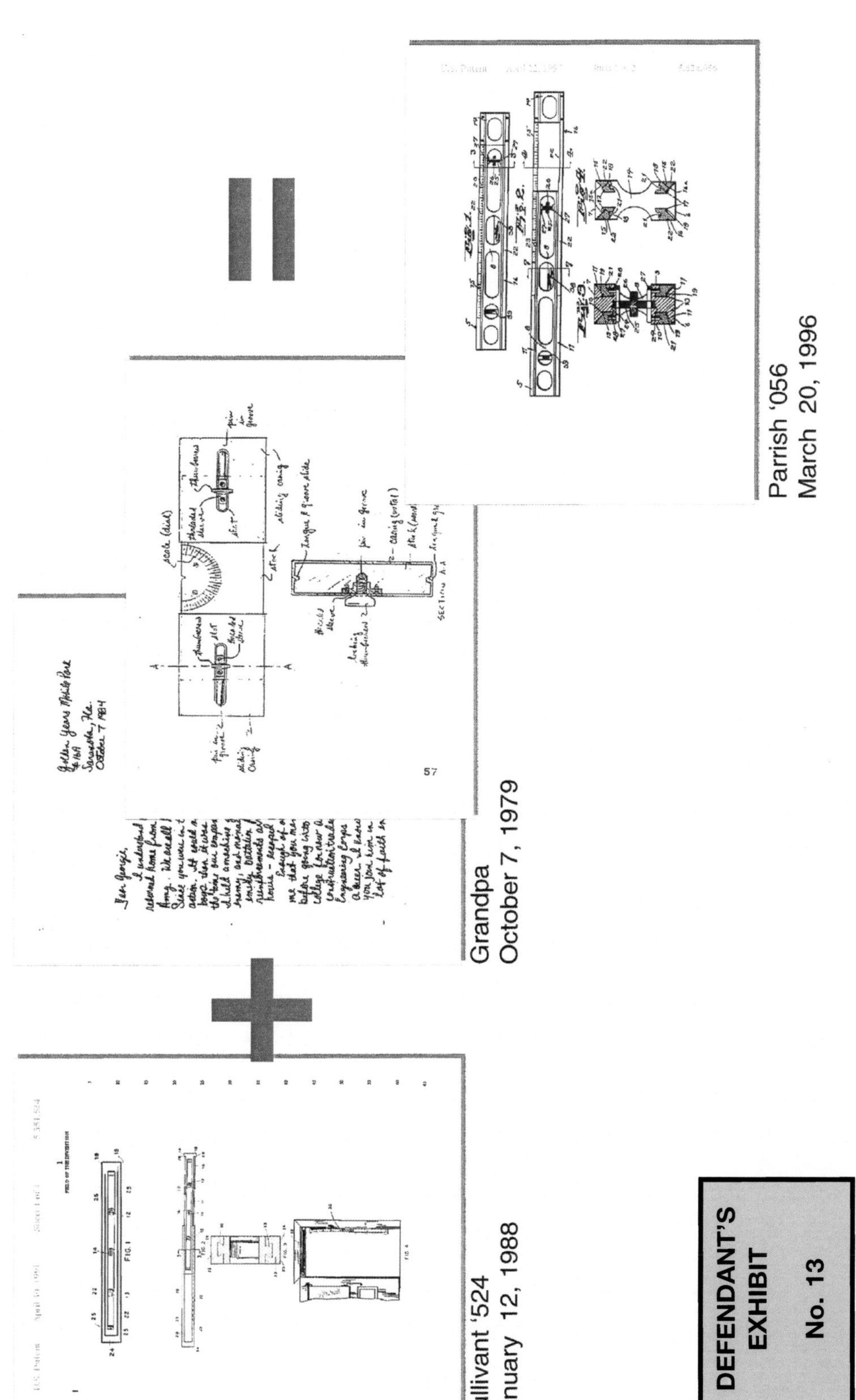

DEFENDANT'S EXHIBIT

No. 13

SECTION I-14

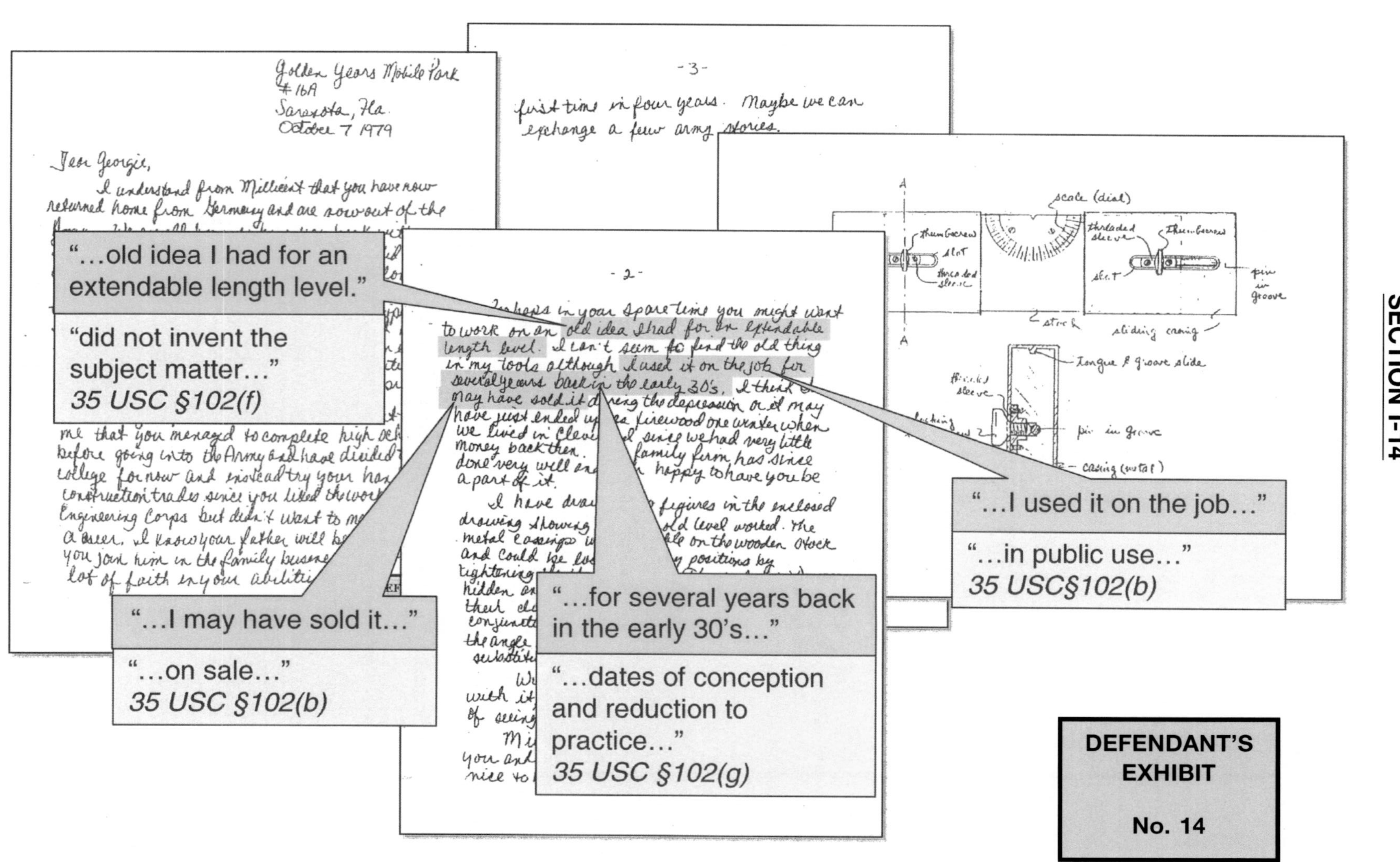
Parrish '056 Invalid
"…old idea I had for an extendable length level."
"did not invent the subject matter…"
35 USC §102(f)
"…I may have sold it…"
"…on sale…"
35 USC §102(b)
"…for several years back in the early 30's…"
"…dates of conception and reduction to practice…"
35 USC §102(g)
"…I used it on the job…"
"…in public use…"
35 USC§102(b)
DEFENDANT'S EXHIBIT
No. 14

SECTION I-15

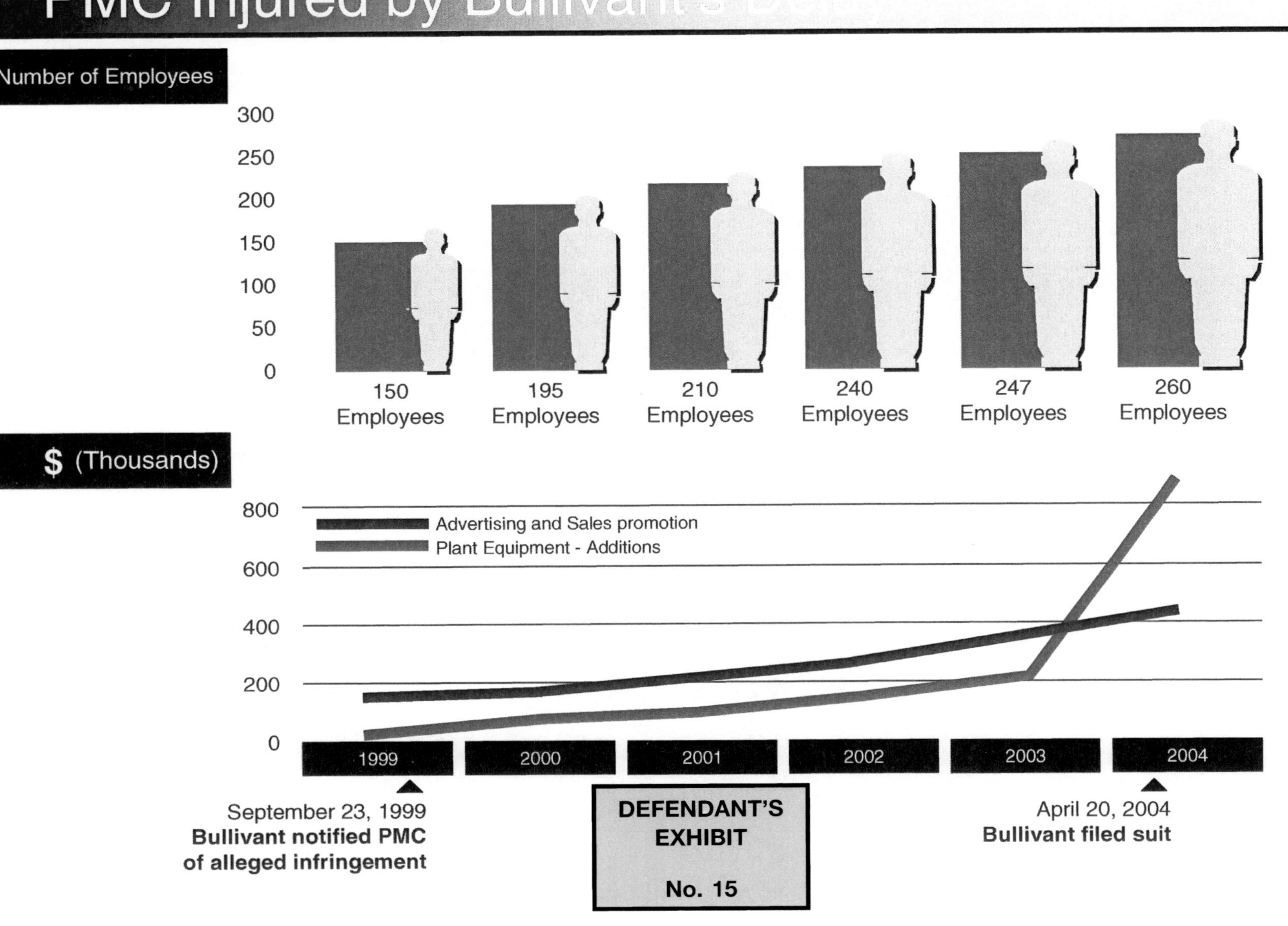

PMC Injured by Bullivant's De
Number of Employees
300
250
200
150
100
50
0
150 Employees
195 Employees
210 Employees
240 Employees
247 Employees
260 Employees
$ (Thousands)
800
600
400
200
0
Advertising and Sales promotion
Plant Equipment - Additions
1999
2000
2001
2002
2003
2004
September 23, 1999
Bullivant notified PMC of alleged infringement
DEFENDANT'S EXHIBIT
No. 15
April 20, 2004
Bullivant filed suit

Section J

Guide to Trial Advocacy Skills

SECTION NO. **Page**

SECTION J-1

INTRODUCTION

The following is designed to provide a brief guide to the basic skills required for trial. Opening statement, direct and cross-examination, impeachment, introduction of exhibits, handling of expert witnesses, *Markman* proceedings, and closing argument are covered. These materials do not presume to contain all the information available on these subjects. Numerous books and research articles have been written on trial techniques and skills. These publications are more thorough and provide many more examples than could possibly be included in these materials.

Several of these publications were very helpful in the preparation of these materials, and citations to pertinent sections of these publications appear at the end of each section. The following publications are recommended for their readability, examples, and practical approach to trial practice.

Lubet, Steven, *Modern Trial Advocacy Analysis and Practice* (3rd Ed.), National Institute for Trial Advocacy, 2004.

Bergman, Paul, *Trial Advocacy* (4th Ed.), West Nutshell Series, December, 2006.

Mauet, Thomas A., *Trial Techniques* (7th Ed.), Aspen Publishers, 2007.

SECTION J-2

OPENING STATEMENTS

The obvious purpose of the opening statement is to provide the factfinder with a synopsis of the case, but the opening statement is also the opportunity to establish the theme of the case and to put the factfinder in a receptive mood to listen to your evidence.

The standard description of the opening is "a summary of the evidence to be produced by the maker of the statement." This means that the opening statement should be based upon anticipated witness testimony and documentary and real evidence. The attorneys' inferences and conclusions from that evidence should be saved for closing argument.

This is not to say that the opening statement has to be a boring recitation of witnesses and facts. The opening should be told dramatically, making certain to "weave into the tale" the important places, people, issues, and expected conclusion of the case. The lawyer's attitude while delivering the opening should be confident, not tentative: "we will prove," not "we hope to be able to prove." The use of charts or other demonstrative aids should be considered to add interest to the presentation, although the rules on the use of exhibits during openings vary from jurisdiction to jurisdiction and judge to judge.

Capture the factfinder's attention by highlighting the most relevant facts with short, compelling, impact statements. Avoid technical tedium and be sure to humanize your client. At the same time, because patent cases are complex, opening statements should refer to the law and help the factfinder orient to the inquiries at hand.

> **Practice Pointer:**
>
> ***Convey command of the case and demonstrate your trustworthiness to the factfinder. Establish your integrity and confidence from the outset.***

Be careful not to make binding admissions in the opening, thereby conceding parts of your opponent's case, and remember that the opening must state enough of the evidence to overcome a motion to dismiss or a motion for nonsuit.

Although the opening statement could theoretically include every witness, all the expected testimony, and those expected to testify, such an approach would overwhelm the jury (and probably bore them terribly). State the important testimony from the main witnesses, without attempting to tie every statement to a specific witness. In this way, there will be fewer "promises" to keep to the judge or jury throughout the trial—should the testimony that unfolds differ from that which was anticipated, the judge or jury may not even be aware of the differences.

> **Practice Pointer:**
>
> ***Make it simple—speak in plain English, be concise, and incorporate a select few timelines, demonstratives, and/or exhibits.***

The opening statement should be concise but detailed enough to state your case, and of course, should not be argumentative. Save the argument for closing.

Lubet,	Chapter 12
Bergman,	Chapter 6
Mauet,	Chapter 4

SECTION J-3

DIRECT EXAMINATION

The goals of direct examination are to present the evidence that is legally sufficient, to raise each claim or defense of your case, to create a record for appeal, and to convince the factfinder of the truthfulness of the testimony of your witnesses. How should the direct examination be conducted to achieve these goals? First, the lawyer must have total control of the direct examination—witnesses should be thoroughly prepared before trial. This preparation should include the topics to be covered, the specific questions in the most important areas, and the questions that could be asked on cross-examination.

Although the direct examination should be lawyer-controlled, the factfinder's focus must be on the witness and the witness's telling of his or her story. It is more persuasive if the witness tells the evidence, rather than confirming what the lawyers asks. Therefore, use open, non-leading questions. This will allow the witness to do most of the talking. The questions should be brief, using lay language whenever possible. Avoid compound questions and questions with negatives to minimize the potential for confusion.

> **Practice Pointer:**
>
> ***Use thematic organization, eliciting your strongest facts at the beginning and end of the examination.***

In organizing the direct examination, remember the recency-primacy theory. After preliminary questions have been answered, go immediately to questions that relate to an important issue in the case, and have an important point on which to end the examination.

Consider also how to organize the testimony around these "strong" points. Do you want a chronological account of the events, since chronological order is easiest to follow? Could the testimony be structured by topics, and then chronologically within each topic? How can you structure the testimony to both hold the attention of the factfinder and still logically recount the facts?

> **Practice Pointer:**
>
> ***Articulate headings and transitions to help the factfinder understand how the testimony is organized.***

Whatever organization is used, help the factfinder track and remember the testimony. Be certain the witness gives as much detail as necessary to ensure that the testimony is understandable, but avoid eliciting unnecessary details that can bury strong points. Because key information is more likely to be remembered if it is reinforced verbally and visually, consider the use of charts or other demonstrative aids to make the testimony more interesting and comprehensible to the judge or jury.

Lubet,	Chapter 4
Bergman,	Chapter 7
Mauet,	Chapter 5

SECTION J-4

EXHIBITS

In laying a foundation for the introduction of exhibits and demonstrative evidence, there are five areas to consider. Only relevance and authentication must be dealt with for each exhibit or demonstrative, but you should always run a mental checklist against the foundation that has been laid.

1. AUTHENTICATION—Is the exhibit or demonstrative evidence what it purports to be? See Federal Rule 901 for authentication requirements for various matters.
2. RELEVANCY—Is the exhibit or demonstrative evidence relevant to some issue in the case?
3. HEARSAY—Is the exhibit or demonstrative evidence hearsay? If so, does it qualify under an exception to the hearsay rule? See Federal Rule 803.
4. BEST EVIDENCE—Is the proposed exhibit the "best evidence" when required? Federal Rule 1002 requires the original only to prove the contents of a "writing, record or photograph," unless otherwise provided by the rules. See Federal Rule 1001 for the definitions and Federal Rule 1003 for the admissibility of duplicates as originals.
5. PRIVILEGE—Are there any privileges, such as doctor-patient, attorney-client, or accountant-client that might preclude the use of the evidence?

> **Practice Pointer:**
>
> ***Memorize foundational litanies to internalize the components of a sufficient evidentiary foundation.***

The actual mechanics of introducing exhibits and demonstrative evidence are just that: mechanics. The same procedures, even the same words, should be used every time a substantive exhibit or demonstrative evidence is to be admitted. It is best to cover general foundation requirements before the witness is handed the exhibit. For example, the business procedure for handling incoming and outgoing correspondence should be testified to before the witness is asked to look at a particular piece of correspondence. In the same manner, general testimony concerning a relevant intersection should be elicited before the diagram is produced.

Keep in mind that foundational testimony can satisfy both technical and persuasive goals. Technical foundation is required to build a sufficient evidentiary record. However, foundational testimony can also inform the factfinder about the importance, *vel non,* of an exhibit or demonstrative. For example, although admission of an original U.S. patent document is a simple technical matter, the patent owner can persuasively underscore the patent's importance and presumption of validity by reviewing the patent prosecution process and highlighting the gold seal and colorful ribbon indicating the United States Patent and Trademark Office's approval.

Once you are ready to deal specifically with the exhibit, the procedure is as follows:

1. HAVE THE ITEM MARKED AS AN EXHIBIT FOR IDENTIFICATION PURPOSES—In the federal courts, exhibits are normally premarked.
2. PROVIDE A COPY OF THE EXHIBIT TO OPPOSING COUNSEL.
3. ASK PERMISSION TO APPROACH THE WITNESS—"Your Honor, may I approach the witness?" This is not required in all jurisdictions, but, even when it is not required, it is still a good procedure to follow.
4. HAND THE EXHIBIT TO THE WITNESS AND HAVE WITNESS EXAMINE IT—"I hand you what has been (previously) marked as plaintiff's Exhibit 1 for identification and ask you to examine it." *REMEMBER:* Until an exhibit is introduced into evidence, it should be referred to as an exhibit for identification.

5. HAVE THE WITNESS IDENTIFY THE EXHIBIT, WITHOUT TESTIFYING TO ITS CONTENTS—This can be done with a leading question, "Is this the letter about which you have previously testified?," or with a non-leading question, "Do you recognize this?" "Without testifying to the contents, what is it?" Of course, on direct, the witness must be prepared to give a complete response to this question.
6. AUTHENTICATE THE EXHIBIT AS REQUIRED BEYOND THE IDENTIFICATION.
7. MOVE THE EXHIBIT INTO EVIDENCE—"We offer plaintiff's exhibit 1 for identification into evidence."
8. SHOW TO THE JURY IN SOME WAY—Once the exhibit has been admitted, use it. Consider in advance how to most persuasively publish the exhibit—will call outs and highlights using trial presentation software or a document camera suffice, or should each member of the jury hold and examine the exhibit?

For photographs, diagrams, and other "representative" evidence, before moving the exhibit into evidence you must ask the witness, "Is this a fair and accurate representation of _______?" (Fill in the blank with whatever the exhibit purports to represent.)

Remember that you are generating a written transcript. References to exhibits and to portions of exhibits must be express and specific. Be sure that you or the witness indicate on the record what is being reviewed/discussed/annotated. For example, expressly direct the witness's attention "to page 5, line 14 of Plaintiff's Exhibit 7," instead of "that page." On post-trial motions or appeal, a written record devoid of specific references to the evidentiary record will be of little assistance.

Before utilizing demonstrative evidence, you must show that the exhibit would aid the witness in explaining his testimony or aid the jury in understanding that testimony.

Lubet,	Chapter 10
Bergman,	Chapter 8
Mauet,	Chapter 6

SECTION J-5

CROSS-EXAMINATION

When a lawyer cross-examines a witness, she does so for at least one of the following reasons: 1) to discredit (impeach) testimony, either of that witness or of other witnesses; 2) to corroborate testimony favorable to her own case; or 3) to elicit independent evidence that is favorable to her own case. If at least one of these objectives cannot be accomplished, consider *not* cross-examining the witness. (Impeachment is discussed in a separate section. This section is a general discussion on conducting an effective cross-examination.)

It is imperative that the lawyer have total control during the cross-examination. Because the lawyer cannot prepare the witness or depend upon the witness's cooperation, this control is most often achieved by the form of the questions; specifically, use leading questions during cross-examination whenever possible. (For inexperienced lawyers, this means *always* use leading questions on cross-examination.) Remember: A leading question is one that suggests the answer. By using leading questions, the lawyer is telling the witness what to say.

There are three basic "don'ts" of cross-examination. As with everything, there are exceptions to these rules, but departure from these rules is risky for even the most experienced trial lawyer.

1. DON'T ASK A QUESTION TO WHICH YOU DO NOT KNOW THE ANSWER.
2. DON'T ASK WHY (unless you *know* the answer to the "why" and can prove that answer by independent evidence, or the answer to "why" does not matter).
3. DON'T ASK THE "ULTIMATE" QUESTION. Do not ask the witness on cross to give you the conclusion you need to win your case. You will not get it. Ask the questions that lead to the conclusion, but save the conclusion for your closing argument.

One final point. Choose two to three areas in which to question the witness on cross, and then sit down. Use short, incremental, leading statements, and ensure the witness agrees or disagrees as dictated by your statement. Be deliberate and be brief—the longer the cross-examination, the more opportunity the witness has to say something you do not want to hear. The best way to present your case is normally through your own witnesses.

Lubet, Chapter 5
Bergman, Chapter 9
Mauet, Chapter 7

SECTION J-6

IMPEACHMENT

One of the purposes of cross-examination is to impeach the witness. Successful impeachment makes the witness appear less credible to the jury. Under the Federal Rules of Evidence, any witness can be impeached by any party (Federal Rule 607).

Before a witness is impeached, there are two things that must be determined. First, what is the net effect of the witness's testimony? If the net effect is favorable to your client, it is unwise to proceed with the impeachment. There is no need to discredit a favorable witness. The second consideration is whether or not the impeachment will be successful. Impeachment is an indictment of the witness. If the impeachment fails or appears petty, the witness's standing and credibility may be improved. If impeachment is to be used, it should be aimed at important parts of the testimony and have a high probability of being successful. Avoid the "instinct for the capillary."

There are numerous areas for impeachment. The most common are:

1. PERCEPTION—This is the first area in which to look for errors with eyewitnesses. Physical circumstances, distractions, and psychological factors can influence a witness's perception of an event. These areas can be pursued on cross-examination.
2. RECOLLECTION/RETENTION—The witness's memory of the event can be attacked in several ways. Passage of time normally obscures details. It can also be shown that this was a routine event—nothing happened at the time to make the event memorable, so the witness is not testifying to that event, but to the routine (*e.g.*, a secretary typing a letter and a carbon). Similarly, blurred memory can be shown because of countless *similar events* (*e.g.*, accident investigations for policemen).
3. COMMUNICATION/SOURCE OF KNOWLEDGE—Is the witness testifying from personal knowledge or from what others have told him? Reliance on hearsay is obviously objectionable. Furthermore, if the witness sounds "rehearsed," the questions on cross should center around the number of times the witness has talked with other people about his testimony.
4. BIAS, PREJUDICE, INTEREST, CORRUPTION—These areas of impeachment require some development on cross-examination if they are to be effective. The ability to develop these areas will be determined by whether the questions are collateral to the issues in the case. If the questions are collateral, the examiner is bound by the witness's answer. Otherwise, other evidence or testimony will be allowed to prove the bias, prejudice, interest, or corruption.
5. PRIOR CRIMINAL RECORD—Under the Federal Rules, criminal records can be used to impeach only if the crime was punishable by death or by imprisonment for more than one year *and* the probative value outweighs the prejudicial effect, *or* it is a crime involving a "dishonest or false" statement. In addition, the conviction may not be used if ten years have elapsed from the date of the conviction or release from imprisonment for that crime (whichever is later), unless the probative value outweighs the prejudicial effect. There is no time limit for the use of convictions for "dishonest or false statements" (Federal Rule 609).
6. PRIOR BAD ACTS—Use of this type of impeachment varies significantly from jurisdiction to jurisdiction. Under the Federal Rules, prior bad acts may be used as impeachment only if the prior bad acts bear some relationship to credibility. No extrinsic evidence is permitted on this point [Federal Rule 608(b)].

7. PRIOR INCONSISTENT STATEMENTS—This is the most common form of impeachment. The prior inconsistent statement may be either oral or written. Under the Federal Rules, the statement does not have to be disclosed to the witness prior to the impeachment, although written statements must be shown to opposing counsel upon request (Federal Rule 613).

Even though the statement need not be disclosed, a foundation must be laid before using a prior statement. Before the statement is used, the witness should be bound to his present testimony. This is accomplished by clearly identifying the statements made on direct that are to be challenged. Then the witness should be asked to recall the taking of a deposition or the fact of making the statement in question.

Next, elicit the circumstances involved in making the earlier statement. For oral statements, this means directing the witness's attention to the date, time, and place of the statement. For written statements, have the witness recall reading, making corrections if required, and signing the statement. For depositions, also verify that the deposition was taken under oath, with opposing counsel present, that both lawyers asked questions, that the answers were recorded, that the witness read the transcript and could correct errors, and that the witness signed the deposition. Whenever possible, have the witness identify his/her signature confirming that she reviewed the deposition transcript or otherwise authored the earlier statement.

Once the statement has been authenticated, continue with the impeachment by reading the statement and asking the witness to agree that it was her statement.

8. REPUTATION—Impeaching a witness's reputation is not done by cross-examination of that witness, but by calling another witness who can testify to the first witness's reputation in the community *and* give his own opinion of the reputation of the first witness. Under the Federal Rules, only testimony concerning reputation for truthfulness is admissible [Federal Rule 608(a)].
9. IMPEACHMENT BY TESTIMONY INCONSISTENT WITH OTHER WITNESSES'S TESTIMONY—A witness may be impeached by demonstrating inconsistencies between his testimony and the testimony of other witnesses in the case. If the inconsistencies are between the testimony of two of the opponent's witnesses, showing the inconsistency will emphasize the contradiction to the factfinder. If, on the other hand, the inconsistencies are between your witness's testimony and the testimony of the opponent's witness, there is little to be gained by highlighting the differences, because everyone expects witnesses from opposite sides to have different versions of the events.

In addition, consider the significance of the inconsistency to the case. If it is a trivial point, there is little gain and some risk in emphasizing the inconsistency, since the factfinder may decide that the lawyer is attempting to obfuscate the issues through the questioning.

Lubet,	Chapter 6
Bergman,	pp. 324–338
Mauet,	Section 7.7

SECTION J-7

EXPERT WITNESSES

When should an expert witness be used? The Federal Rules provide the answer in Federal Rule 702:

> If scientific, technical, or other specialized knowledge will assist the trier of fact to understand the evidence or to determine a fact in issue, a witness qualified as an expert by knowledge, skill, training, or education may testify thereto in the form of an opinion or otherwise.

When expert testimony is to be used, the attorney must work closely with the expert in preparing that portion of the case, so that the attorney becomes an "expert" in that area of knowledge required for the case. It is imperative that this knowledge be acquired if you are to conduct a cross-examination of the opposing counsel's expert, as well as handle the direct examination of your own expert.

How do you decide whom to use as the expert? First, decide what credentials would lend the greatest credence to the expert opinion. Should the expertise be "on-the-job" or academic? An academic expert may not appear as credible in his testimony about the daily operation of a piece of equipment as the expert who has been operating and repairing similar equipment for the past twenty years.

Patent cases almost always involve one or more issues that must be viewed from the perspective of a "person having ordinary skill in the art" at the time of the patented invention. Thus, for some issues, it may be important that the expert have at least the requisite skill level during the relevant time period.

> **Practice Pointer:**
>
> ***Good experts are good teachers. Choose someone who speaks and communicates well and can effectively use graphics, models, animations, etc.***

Has the expert previously testified or taken a public position with respect to the type of opinion he would be asked to give in this case? Preferably, your expert should be someone whose previous statements are consistent with the opinion you will elicit.

Finally, because you can usually choose your expert from many capable people, the person you choose should be someone with a good "court presence"—a person who acts as a professional but who is not condescending, and someone who is able to reduce technical terminology to layman's terms. This last point is critical. If your expert is unable to make his or her testimony understandable to the factfinder, the examination is merely an exercise in futility.

How should the expert testimony be constructed? First, the witness must be qualified as an expert. Testimony must be given to show the expert's professional credentials, both generally in his field and specifically as they relate to expertise in the issues of this case. Counsel sometimes will stipulate to the credentials of opposing experts, hoping that impressive credentials will not be developed at trial. This way, the factfinder does not become too impressed with the expert's credentials. Even with a stipulation as to credentials, spend some time developing the witness's background as a foundation to the basis for his or her opinions. After the witness's expertise has been established, and in courts that so require, tender the witness to the court as an expert in whatever field is dictated by the qualifying testimony.

Next you must establish how this expert's testimony is relevant to the issues at trial, if that was not accomplished during the earlier part of the testimony.

Now, the basis for the expert opinion should be established. Under Federal Rule 703, the information used to support the expert opinion may be information that is "reasonably relied upon by experts in the particular field." The facts of the particular case may be perceived by the expert or told to him, at or before the time of the hearing.

Federal Rule 705 allows the expert to state his or her opinion and reasons for that opinion without disclosing the basis on direct, unless required to do so by the judge. However, the better strategy is to elicit this testimony on direct examination to make his opinions more credible to the jury.

When the expert is asked his opinion, the question should be separate, clear, and dramatic:

Q. Based upon all the materials you have reviewed, and the education and training you have described, have you reached an opinion as to the cause of John Bravon's paralysis?
A. Yes.
Q. What is that opinion?

The expert need not have personal knowledge of the facts to give his opinion (Federal Rule 703). He may even give an opinion on the ultimate issue (Federal Rule 704). Remember, however, that the further removed an expert's background and experience is from the issues at hand, the more likely it becomes that the expert will be attacked on cross-examination and/or that your opponent will ask the court to exercise its gatekeeping functions to limit or exclude the expert's testimony.

The actual mechanics of direct and cross-examination of an expert are the same as those for any other witness, although some additional tools are available, such as the use of "learned treatises" under Federal Rule of Evidence 803(18). In addition, more so than with fact witnesses, experts should be asked to support or defend their opinions using demonstratives. Effective experts will be able to communicate opinions in simple words and with memorable images. Much has been written on handling experts both on direct and cross. It is recommended that you read several of these discussions to learn the fine points of this skill.

Lubet,	Chapter 8
Bergman,	Chapter 10
Mauet,	Chapter 8

SECTION J-8

MARKMAN CLAIM CONSTRUCTION PROCEEDINGS

Unique to patent cases is the role of the district court in construing the meaning of a patent's claims and, thus, determining what the patent covers or doesn't cover [*Markman v. Westview Instruments, Inc.*, 52 F.3d 967, 979–81 (Fed. Cir. 1995) (*en banc*), *aff'd,* 517 U.S. 370 (1996)]. This "*Markman*" process is often case dispositive, yet the litigants' involvement in claim construction varies from court to court and even from judge to judge within a district.

Courts with special local patent rules often require the parties to exchange detailed claim construction positions and agree to the meaning of as many claim terms as possible before anything is submitted to the court. Generally, courts require written briefs setting forth proposed claim constructions along with the evidence supporting each proposed claim construction. In some courts the patent owner submits the first brief and the alleged infringer responds, while in other courts the alleged infringer submits the first brief and the patent owner replies. In yet other courts the litigants simultaneously exchange opening and response briefs. Some courts request introductory technology summaries, and some will appoint experts to aid the court in understanding very complex technologies.

Many judges conduct *Markman* hearings during which evidence is presented and witnesses testify. Some judges simply request an oral argument during which counsel address arguments from the briefs. Because judges use these proceedings to learn about the patented technology, about the state of the art at the time of the invention, and about the evidence relevant to the patent claims, counsel should approach the entire *Markman* process as a potentially case dispositive mini-trial.

Counsel should discuss claim construction logistics during initial case management conferences and seek guidance from the court regarding the protocols that will be applied. Knowing when and how the court will construe the claims informs counsel's strategy and phasing of fact and expert discovery, and can help the parties anticipate opportunities for seeking summary judgment or settlement. Following are general considerations relevant to *Markman* claim construction briefs and arguments.

Markman Claim Construction Briefs

1. CRITICALLY ANALYZE AND APPLY THE LAW—Claim construction case law can be extremely nuanced, and familiar canons of claim construction may be applied in disparate ways depending on the facts at hand. Careful and thorough legal research is essential.
2. FOCUS ON THE INTRINSIC RECORD FIRST—Claims are to be construed with preferential reliance on intrinsic evidence, namely, the words and figures used in the patent and the record reflecting the patent's application and process to issuance (the "prosecution history"). The court may consider extrinsic evidence, but it is not the starting point.
3. SIMPLIFY—Establish consistent nomenclature, color codes, references, and other tools to help the court understand the patent and your proposed claim constructions. Ensure that your briefs are well-organized and understandable.
4. MAKE IT VISUAL—Magnify, color, and annotate the patent's figures, and include the annotated illustrations directly in the text of your brief. Compare and contrast statements from the intrinsic and/or extrinsic record using side-by-side illustrations in the brief. Consider working with a professional graphic design firm to create graphic aids for the brief and hyperlinked, searchable evidence and animations that can be submitted to the court on DVD.

MARKMAN CLAIM CONSTRUCTION ARGUMENTS

1. ANTICIPATE THE COURT'S QUESTIONS—Prepare to answer questions from the court, the judge's clerk, and any court-appointed expert. Outline your presentation in a logical flow, but remain flexible to address the court's questions immediately and succinctly. When directing the court's attention to aspects of the briefs or evidence in the record that support your argument, do so with specificity, just like at trial.
2. BEWARE OF ADMISSIONS—Judges use claim construction hearings and arguments to test alternative claim constructions and to gauge the strength of the proposed claim constructions. Avoid making statements that modify your proposed constructions or agreeing with court-proposed alternative constructions, unless you have previously, thoroughly considered the impact of such admissions and know how they affect the infringement and invalidity positions of the parties.
3. ROADMAP AND TRANSITION—Claim construction issues can be factually and legally complex. Let the court know what your argument is about, where you are at in that argument, and where you are going. When switching topics to answer the court's questions, advise the court how various arguments fit together and alert the court that you are switching topics.
4. MAKE IT VISUAL—Build on the visuals submitted with your brief and create additional visuals to address those used by your opponent. Prepare to use exhibits, graphics, and animations throughout your argument by using a combination of pre-prepared demonstratives (*e.g.*, presentation slides, animations, etc.) as well as illustrative aids that you can manipulate or build during the argument (*e.g.*, paper exhibits, physical products, models, etc.).

Successful *Markman* claim construction proceedings are founded on thorough preparation and organization. The more clearly and simply you can articulate a proposed construction that is consistent with the evidentiary record and supported by controlling law, the more likely it is that the court will construe the claims the way you propose.

SECTION J-9

CLOSING ARGUMENT

Persuasion is the watchword of an effective closing argument. The primary purpose of a closing argument is to put the evidence into a cohesive form that is persuasive to the factfinder. To be persuasive, the closing argument must explain the meaning and significance of the evidence as the evidence supports the claims of your client. You must show the factfinder how helpful inferences are drawn from the evidence in your client's favor and how unhelpful inferences that will be argued by your opponent are incorrect or inconsequential.

The closing argument must be prepared before the trial begins. The entire trial should be molded around the closing argument. The issues and themes argued at closing must be developed throughout the rest of the trial. Just as preparation is the key to being a successful trial lawyer, pretrial preparation of the closing argument is the key to a successful trial.

How is a closing argument structured? Entire books have been devoted to this question, so it would be presumptuous to attempt to provide a definitive answer in these materials. There are some general guidelines to consider, however, when preparing a closing argument:

1. KNOW YOURSELF, AND KNOW YOUR JUDGE AND JURY—The closing argument reflects the lawyer's personality more than any other stage of the trial. To be persuasive, the delivery of the closing argument must be convincing. The judge or jury must be persuaded that you believe in the argument. If you are not an emotional person, or have not appeared to be emotional throughout the trial, will a highly emotional closing be believable? Likely not. The closing argument must be consistent with the lawyer's personality as presented in the courtroom throughout the trial.
2. CREATE A MOOD—This is the most overlooked aspect of closings, but creating a mood is vital to the persuasiveness of the argument. The mood should be established at the very beginning of the argument, when jurors and judges are most attentive. Decide how the factfinder should "feel" about the case, and be certain that such a mood prevails throughout the argument. In the process, create a moral imperative that dictates a finding in your client's favor. A bench trial requires this even more than a jury trial, if you are to keep the judge's attention throughout.

   In creating a mood, be aware of the various principles of persuasion or psychological devices that can make the closing argument more persuasive, such as theories of recency and primacy, which state that people remember best what they hear or see first and last in any presentation. Items in the middle tend to get lost. An effective closing, then, is one with strong points at the beginning and end of the argument.

   Believability is also enhanced if the argument is structured in a climax-anticlimax form. Argue the positive points of the case initially, so the factfinder can be convinced. Then, if the need exists, deal with the negative aspects of the case. It is more difficult to change an established belief (what the factfinder heard first), so tell the judge/jury what they should believe at the beginning of the argument.
3. SIMPLIFY THE ISSUES—Regardless of the type of case, strive to state the issues clearly and simply. Stress only key issues in the closing argument. The issues will be easier to understand and the argument will be more persuasive.
4. REITERATE YOUR THEME—The theme is separate from the issues in the case. It is the "moral" rationale of the case. In personal injury cases involving

traffic accidents, the plaintiff's theme is often "keeping the public highways safe." In commercial cases, someone is always "preserving the free enterprise system." The theme should provide the trier-of-fact with a reason, founded in human experience, to decide for your client. Your entire trial story, from opening through witness testimony to closing, should consistently reflect the theme of your case. Closing argument is the lawyer's opportunity to connect the thematic dots pointing to a singular conclusion—a verdict in your client's favor.

5. BE SPECIFIC—Do not argue generalities. The factfinder must have specific evidence upon which a decision can be based. Quote important testimony exactly. Refer to exhibits and portions of exhibits with specificity. Recall key demonstratives and use them during your argument.
6. USE EXHIBITS—You add interest and emphasis by using your best exhibits during closing, especially since the jurors will have that same evidence in the jury room.
7. REHEARSE THE LAST TWO MINUTES THOROUGHLY—If you are under time constraints, it is crucial to have the last two minutes of your argument well in your mind, almost memorized, no matter how you handle the rest of the argument. This will ensure that you will end your argument on a strong, positive point that will be convincing.

What are some of the techniques to use in constructing closing arguments? Every successful lawyer has a favorite technique to use in closing. Ask other lawyers what they use, or listen to some closing arguments to see what you think is effective. Here are some of the techniques:

1. ANALOGY—The use of analogies is very persuasive. The analogy is intended to help the factfinder equate the case with an everyday experience or a well-known maxim. Aesop's Fables are often used, as are stories from "real" life. In circumstantial evidence cases, the analogy is made to the child with cookie crumbs on his mouth who denies eating the cookies. (Often it becomes the lawyer's child, just yesterday.) Look for stories and jot them down. You never know when they might be incorporated into a closing argument.
2. UNDERSTATEMENT—A persuasive argument "suggests" some of its conclusions. Factfinders want to think the decision was their own deduction. Urge the fact finder to make that deduction; imply, without explicit statement, the conclusions they will have to make.

The important thing to remember is that there are no "good" or "bad" closing arguments, only persuasive or unpersuasive ones.

Lubet,	Chapter 13
Bergman,	Chapter 11
Mauet,	Chapter 9

Index

Notes

Notes

Notes

Notes

Notes